1

SETTLE: A FAMILY JOURNEY THROUGH SLAVERY

BY CHARLES D. RODENBOUGH

Dedicated to Washington, a slave and all he could have been.

For eighty-five years we have been hung on slavery's cross and been whistling through the dark in the hope that a miracle would save us.

Judge George Howard

April 14, 1861 - On the road between Danbury and Madison

TABLE OF CONTENTS

Preface   8

Illustrations   11

Book I - Prelude-Highway Marker J-114   13

Book II - The Douglas Inheritance   21

Book III - Washington, a Slave   67

Book IV - My Intended Wife and Children   73   *Badly written!*

Book V - Thomas Settle, Unionist   105

Book VI – Impeachment   137

Book VII - Joe   159

Book VIII - Nubbin Ridge   173

Teaching Supplement   181

Editor's Notes   201

Bibliography   214

PREFACE

The family that ignites this story and connects the disparity in the varying structures within it, is the Settle family in North Carolina, Tennessee, Ohio and the nation. The themes are slavery and multiculturalism. The time spans from the antebellum 19th century to the 21st century when America has an African American President.

No matter what part of that nearly 200 years in which you lived or about which you have read, it is difficult to see while immersed, the cyclical repetition being played out. The emotional depth of that theme seems to demand either prejudice or indifference from the reader or hearer. Absorbed in the reading of a book or the viewing of an electronic device, it is possible only to deal with the moment in such a way as to carry from one sequence to another and to attempt to link sequences. In such circumstances, it is bilateral history. It can be made academically accurate by the inclusion of footnotes. Unfortunately it also tends to be myopic.

So, what is there in this presentation that improves on our ability to more broadly understand the subject and to see more clearly the influences at play on all the characters? First of all is time. History is not static although at times, when in a text, it seems to be self contained in a moment. A date may anchor an event but it does nothing to interpret the circumstances. Secondly we have people. History features the most famous, often ignoring the myriad levels of the society. Or history tends to examine a class or race at a distance from the significant events that subtly bear influence on the choices available to those groups. Then, there is distance. History matures with perspective. Too close to the event, or too far away from it, can skew the lens. History, written particularly close to a civil upheaval, usually absorbs disproportionate amounts of prejudice, pride, grief, and malice - all factors that are abrasive to good judgment or an objective evaluation of justice.

This story was written over an extended period, in diverse original forms. Only after I had studied and reviewed the parts, did I recognize a conscious thread that was worth considering. It was a good matrix for observing slavery in a particular part of the South and to look at it from its roots to the disruptive strain of influence in the United States from the point at which our early laws accepted race and not ethnicity to identify what was African. Once laws recognized color in terms of one drop of black blood, or some variation of that standard, the African was established as a "they" of society. Ethnicity also sets people apart but it becomes theoretically absorbed in the melting pot.

This book offers history as a series of concentric circles. The story of Senator Stephen A. Douglas' political dilemma concerning the ownership of slaves, demonstrates that at the highest level of American government, men of good will had difficulty in functioning within the bounds of an ethical contradiction. The family of Josiah and Nancy Ann Graves Settle outlines the anguish and inconsistency within a single family in mediating humanity. Thomas Settle, Robert Martin Douglas, and Josiah Thomas Settle illustrate three lives, in an extended family, that interact upon and have to interface with, the flotsam and jetsam of slavery. Nubbin Ridge is the link to the possibilities of a new national dynamic.

In the summer of 2011, I was informed that my friend, Robert Dick Douglas, had told his family that he would like to visit the Settle Cemetery on his 99th birthday. I made the arrangements with Bob Carter and a company of about a dozen arrived at the cemetery in late morning on a beautiful summer day. This was the same cemetery that is central to this story and it contained so many of the members of Dick Douglas' family. I believe that visit, and the joy we had as this exuberant gentleman regaled us with stories and events he had picked up over a period of almost a hundred years of family history, that was the seed of this book.

The cemetery was on part of the Sauratown. Although my work has yet to absolutely match the Sauratown slaves with the Settle story, it seems only natural to view both as contributors to a common historical thread.

Charles D. Rodenbough-2013

ILLUSTRATIONS

Martha Martin Douglas   40

Martin-Douglas graves   44

Robert Martin and Stephen A. Douglas, Jr.   49

Robert Martin Douglas-childhood picture   49

Sen. Stephen A. Douglas   55

Sen. Stephen A. Douglas lying in state   56

Robert Martin house ruins on Dan River   63

Stephen A. Douglas home in Washington   63

Washington a slave, tombstone   69

Thomas Settle, Sr.   78

Henrietta Graves Settle   78

Josiah Settle & tombstone   98

Nancy Ann Graves Settle & tombstone   98

Marriage Record-Josiah Settle and Nancy Ann Graves 103

Governor David Settle Reid at NC Capital   109

Governor David Settle Reid   110

Thomas Settle, Jr.   115

Greensboro lawyers   155

Josiah Thomas Settle   166

Josiah Thomas Settle - Tennessee highway marker   170

Josiah Thomas Settle   170

Josiah Thomas Settle home in Memphis   171

Glen T. Settle program   175

Nubbin Ridge birthplace   175

Wings Over Jordan – TV   178

Wings Over Jordan - Korea 1954   179

GENEALOGY:

Settle-Graves-Douglas genealogy   59

Josiah Settle - mixed race family   76

Martin-Settle genealogy   140

BOOK I
PRELUDE-HIGHWAY MARKER J-114

Chapter 1

The Multicultural Interpretation Committee decided upon Thursday, June 20th, for the dedication, to accommodate working people and avoid conflicts with Sunday and Wednesday church services. They chose 7:00 pm because we could have our program at MARC and then ride up the road to the marker site for the unveiling and still have plenty of light. The plans reflected the effort to get as many African Americans as possible to attend. This dedication was important not least of all as a symbol - the first highway marker in Rockingham County for an African American.

Behind those details lay decades, centuries of suffering and human endeavor, indifferently recorded and dependent on tradition, often politically and socially repressed. The dedication was only the most recent of mile posts on the path of racial compatibility.

Kim came down from her office to find a dozen people already in the entrance lobby of MARC. The mahogany desk furniture appeared as institutionally appropriate for the Museum and Archives of Rockingham County. Some, who had last been in the building, when it was the county courthouse, observed the change from the metal detector and presence of Sheriff's deputies which had formally been necessary for public access to the building.

Flowers on a cadenza were a far cry from the former spare surroundings; and the sprinkling of dressy attire was in obvious contrast to the former presence of nervous families waiting for the trials of their relatives to begin.

The animated advances Kim Rotor carried off when approaching such a gathering, worked well for Rockingham County where most people tended toward the reserved and rarely put themselves out if they were not yet comfortable. The audience that was forming was predominantly black and in an event intentionally organized to be multiracial, it was ordinary to have a reticent reserve until the stage was fully set.

"Are we going to use the orientation room or the court room upstairs?" wondered Joyce Johns, chairperson of the committee.

As if taking her into a confidence, Kim answered behind her hand, "the Genealogy Group already has booked the court room so we will meet down here."

Covering some disappointment, Joyce allowed, "That may be OK. It is better to have to bring in chairs for this room than have too few for the court room."

The organizers shared an uneasy suspense. MARC, from its inception, had made a concerted effort to be a museum and archives for all people in the county. They would make a positive statement that henceforth preservation of history would include all citizens as a real countywide history.

There was no charge for the dedication program but as people arrived, they were asked to sign a guest book with their addresses. Brochures were strategically placed

15

on the glass covered desk-informative ones about the restoration at Wright Tavern, the upcoming 4th of July celebration, and several stacks of membership brochures for the museum. Docents welcomed at the door and manned the desk. Friends chanted and as the lobby filled the first arrivals migrated back along the hall toward the orientation room.

About fifty people filled the seats by 7 pm and folding chairs added another dozen along the walls. The orientation room was formerly a small courtroom. The walls were covered in dark paneled plywood, the floors with an un-intrusive blue carpet. Commanding the room was a mahogany, three level judge's bench surrounded on the second level by recorder's desks, all typical of a definition of legal authority. Adapting such a setting to a public venue for orienting guests for their visit to the museum, was achieved by the large wall screen on which a video looped most of the day. A dedication program for about sixty people crowded onto court benches was less natural. It required the organizers to use the judge's platform in such a way as to indicate to others the most natural positioning on the multi-level platform.

Kim rose to thank everyone for "coming out." She briefly described the evening and then gave formal greetings on behalf of Wentworth Mayor, Dennis Pascal, who had been unable to attend. Kim spoke with her usual enthusiasm pronouncing her words through a smile, that had the effect of couching an upbeat meaning.

Unfortunately, in her whirlwind exclaimers, she stood at the side on the second level of the dais, leaving no clue for the next group as to staging. The First Baptist Church Choir rose next from their scattered positioning in the audience and approached the looming platform each looking fretfully at the others for signs of where to go. When they all had reached the stage, Sterling Barr, the tall grey-haired director, moved tenors and altos around with hand signals until everyone could see him and he them. He reached unobtrusively behind the bar and pushed on the music disc.

An extended pyramid of black-clad singers, harmonized by the music and set in motion by the powerful downbeat of Sterling Barr, erupted into the spiritual, The Storm is Passing Over. The small courtroom was transformed into an event center. Sound and sight, and emotion, took possession in a common human experience no one could, or wanted to, resist. Jubilation! The dream of the theme was verified in music.

Michael Brill, officer in charge of the Highway Marker Program for the North Carolina Department of Archives and History, was overmatched by the choir, the lone man standing after the whirlwind has passed. Not wanting to seem to be pontificating, he chose the lower setting Kim had used to explain the state program that now honored 1600 North Carolinians, dead at least twenty-five years, who had made significant contributions throughout the state or left the state to make a national impact in any field. He had obviously made similar introductions throughout the state over the years attempting on each occasion to be present for the "most important marker yet to be raised." Most sincerely to this group he noted that

17

North Carolina had over 100 markers throughout the state for prominent African Americans but as the first placed in Rockingham County, there was extra importance for this marker to Glenn T. Settle.

Glenn Thomas Settle had been born in 1894 in a rural neighborhood called Nubbin Ridge south of Reidsville. His parents, Reuben and Mary, were sharecroppers, both born to former Rockingham County slaves. Frustrated by the limited opportunity that the rural South offered for his five children, Reuben had moved the family to Pennsylvania. Glenn married and settled in Cleveland, Ohio and found work as a janitor, apartment manager, and truck driver before being ordained as a Baptist minister. In Cleveland in 1935, as minister of the Gethsemane Baptist Church, he organized a choir. He anticipated the potential impact of the popularity of radio and established a weekly program, "The Negro Hour", on Cleveland radio. It was considered the start of the Negro Spiritual Preservation Movement. In January 1938 he debuted his choir nationally over CBS as "Wings Over Jordan." It was the first independently produced national and international radio program created by African Americans.

Standing beside the Judge's bench, Annette Golding seemed small and unassuming. With her head down she paused, then rose to the resounding acapella challenge, "I Been Burked," and the murmurs said, "Oh, Yes!" to the powerful spiritual protest of the enslaved.

Finally, Sterling Barr stood tall before the gathering, switched on his background music and in a baritone voice rich of soul, finished the program with "I've Been in the Storm Too Long." The music itself had been laid out like a memorial to Glenn Settle confirming his early conviction that Negro spirituals were a worthy contribution to the creative richness of the community.

Joyce Johns, before concluding this part of the dedication and in the tone of sharing an aside, said, "In preparing for this day I thought that we should try to contact any members of the Glenn Settle family in Cleveland. In the process and to my complete surprise, I talked with his granddaughter and the President of the "Wings Over Jordan" Alumni Association which is alive and ongoing. Then last Sunday I found out that Glenn still had relatives here in Reidsville and that one of them was sharing my pew that very day. Mrs. Florence Richardson's grandmother was the sister of Glenn Settle's mother."

A reaction of applause and wonderment rippled across the audience. Mrs. Richardson, dressed in a beige hat and summer beige dress with an overwrap, stood up on the side and Kim immediately asked her if she wanted to say anything. With casual grace she moved in front and to the listening ears said, "I want to thank everyone tonight, especially those who have done the research to make this event possible. I never thought I would live to see such a time. I knew Glenn very well. Each year he would return to Reidsville with the "Wings Over Jordan Choir" to give a performance. Of course in those days, blacks were not allowed in hotels so the members of the chorus stayed in individual homes. There was always a great crowd and the newspapers made much of the performances. Now to know

19

that Glenn and his music are going to be honored with this marker is the most wonderful thing I can imagine and I thank you all."

The subsequent formal unveiling of the silver and black highway marker seemed only to punctuate this moment of transformation. One speaker earlier had noted that every time Glenn had been quoted in a public remark about his choir, he had mentioned his desire and hope that all his efforts might be like a bridge. A highway marker only says to a passerby, 'take note. Someone did something of note that needs to be remembered. Someone made a contribution that made your life richer.'

Glenn T. Settle
1894-1967
Founder of Wings Over
Jordan Choir and Negro
Hour Radio show. 1937
He promoted traditional
Spiritual music & racial
harmony. Born 2 mi. SW.

20

BOOK II
THE DOUGLAS
INHERITANCE

Chapter 1

In the courtyard at Bachelor's Hall on a cold February day in 1853, Martha's coffin was loaded for the final time onto the wagon and the tailgate was locked in place. Matthew was seated inside to attend his late mistress as Stephen prepared to mount into the carriage to lead. Mary Martin was seated already in the coach with her two grandsons.

Daniel and Harriet Jones had fed a robust breakfast and, under the circumstances, there had been cordial if reserved conversation. The attention needed to care for the children was a comforting deflection from the melancholy circumstances. Still, adults needed to acknowledge their mourning in words as well as in drab dress. Stephen was the focus in his duality as Senator and widower. In the former role he was a political conciliator of increasing national prominence, destined, many said, to inevitably be President. In the latter, he was a man bereft, consumed by an inexplicable trial. It was this inability to analyze or explain his misfortune that consumed Stephen's consciousness. The arbiter of national compromise could not qualify his own providence.

"Stephen, will you see us on your return. We are very concerned about you and you need to be near friends," said Nancy Jones grasping firmly both of Stephen's hands.
"I haven't thought of a return route, Nancy, and I will be by myself. I would appreciate your hospitality but I plan to go to Raleigh after I leave Rockingham so I am not certain of the final route I will take."

He boarded and the small train of vehicles rolled out onto the Salem-Petersburg Road to the south. "Papa can I ride up front with Henry," asked Robert before they had gone a mile.

"It will be a long trip today," advised his grandmother, "and there will be plenty of time for that." She made no attempt to cover her obvious favoritism for Robert Martin Douglas, named as he was for her late husband. The boy was very disciplined but like his father, he always favored having his next several steps under consideration. He was never capricious seeming to move from one idea or game to another seamlessly and with determination.

The Post Road had been well travelled in Virginia and on this clear day, it seemed destined to be so as they crossed into North Carolina. The Brougham was still new, purchased in the fall so that the family could make these Southern trips in comfort. Stephen and Martha had picked the version with the larger coach because it would carry their entire family. The version of the carriage that had become so very popular in England, since its introduction a decade earlier, had really been for two people and was more fashionable for a city like London. Of course the front seat could fold up when not used and the carriage, like a coach, had an expansive glazed front window behind the coachman's seat. The forewheels could be turned sharply which made for a well controlled ride. Stephen was reminded that he and Martha had intended to have the Douglas and Martin Coats-of-Arms emblazoned on the doors, but now that seemed so trivial.

23

They were crossing the Sauratown, the old Land of Eden of William Byrd and the road followed the Dan River. By now little Stevie was asleep on the front seat and Robert had been allowed to join Henry on the box seat of the driver. Henry always pleased the boy by calling him his footman.

It was such moments, out of earshot of the children, that Stephen Douglas and Mary Martin were able to discuss all the factors that death had used to shift the order of their lives. Both now widowed, they were not able to share their plans as they had with their spouses, but they needed to coordinate plans thinking of the interests of the children.

"I don't think I would have known how to raise a daughter," said Stephen piteously.

"Of course you would have done fine, Stephen, just as you will do fine by the boys. Remember, we all lost Martha and the baby." It was not a scold but a reminder to her son-in-law who was clearly showing signs of becoming morose and self indulgent.

"Why, at such a moment, was it necessary that my wife, their mother, your remaining daughter, should be taken from us all? Martha and my children were part of all my success. People referred to me as Young America and I relished the image because I saw us all as Young America. Did I fly too close to the sun?"

"Stephen, don't be dramatic with me. You may be the "Little Giant" in the eyes of some politicians but you are not Icarus." Mary was plain spoken and she knew her so-in-law tended toward the dramatic and that had set him forward as a politician. No dramatics. No politician. It was

24

time to plan for these boys. Her own heart, cracked by the suddenness of Lucinda's death while she was planning her wedding; and by Robert's death as his plantation in Mississippi was barely organized, had now been surely broken by the loss of Martha in childbirth. Mary Settle Martin had no intention of allowing dramatics or grief to push her world into a ditch. She loved Stephen but after all he was at heart a selfish New England school boy and politics, the higher you go, seems to twist the soul and inflame the ego. She was going to have none of it.

"Mary, you know that I am struggling with myself, my own needs that were nurtured around Martha and the children into a vision so very secure. Without Martha, my image is shattered. It has become an effigy. I can only morn. There is no alternate image in me. I grieve for the children but they are too young to know the depth of their loss and I fear that I do not have the capacity to replenish that loss."

"You had a world within a world - as a Senator and as a man with a family. One complimented the other. Now you fear that without Martha, you have lost your companion but also the harmony of your arrangement. So far you have failed to make a redesign of what you had. My concern is that you cannot use your sons as if they were pawns to some rearrangement. I insist that we consider the best structure for their future. Then you can make whatever adjustments you must make to your life. I don't mean to be insensitive but there has got to be a priority, Stephen."

There was silence for a long while except for the constant muffled dialogue of Henry and Robert on the driver's seat that seemed to accompany all the adult deliberations of words and thoughts.

Stephen meandered through his misery. He had begun January 1853 trying to hold the democrats together. There was sharp division over the program or lack thereof, of the Democratic President, Franklin Pierce. Douglas was being encouraged to take the opportunity to step forward in leadership to secure his own position in 1854. He refused and continued to support the President. Although not yet forty, he had made his opportunity secure with the success of his brokerage of the Compromise of 1850 that had defused a four-year confrontation between the slave and the free states over slavery in new states. He did not have to turn on his President to gain the moment. He had to appear the ever obvious alternative, young, accomplished, a man to approach a very delicate national future. He delivered the dedicatory speech at the unveiling of the equestrian statue of Andrew Jackson before the White House. "Jackson lives in the spirit of the age," he had said, "the genius of progress which is to ennoble and exalt humanity, and preserve and perpetuate liberty." Soon after, news arrived from Illinois that the legislature had elected him to the United States Senate for the second term. To complete his joy, Martha had given birth to a little girl. It seemed to be such complete fulfillment.

Mary Martin ached for the motherless boys. Quivering with the joy of having a new sister, they had suddenly lost her and their dear mother. Robert was about to be four and Stephen Arnold, was just over two. They had a father whose life had been pledged to an electorate. He was a good man but his life was committed to a first priority to constituents and party leadership with demands in Washington and Chicago and Springfield, and two little boys somewhere. She understood that she was the alternative for them all.

"No solution is without negative options," admitted Mary. "The boys need stability, a home without constant shifting locations. Stephen, if you were unencumbered, you might be able to balance some arrangement using nannies. If you were unencumbered! You are not and as far as we can see, you will never be. That is the reality."

"You make me sound like an institution instead of a father."

"You actually approach being an institution in the world that you inhabit," Mary charged matter-of-factly. "You may pretend it is not so when you return to your home but in the past Martha was always there to secure the home setting. She is no longer. I can see that and I am certain you also can, although it is too harsh for you to acknowledge it now. "

Another long pause. They passed the highland prairie of the Sauratown. The view from the coach window was a spread of grassland, trees toward the river and a vivid azure sky. There gaze did not influence their considerations which continued to be about relationships. "Stephen, I am not making a critical judgment. You are a public person and you have a public persona to maintain. Although you are not selfish in your heart, you must think

27

of yourself in order to fulfill your commitment to an electorate. That can never co-exist with a responsibility to raise two young sons on your own." Mary did not need to restate the solution. It had already been proposed many times.

"All the same, I cannot bear to consider the boys living with you in North Carolina so far removed from me," responded Douglas firmly. It seemed that as long as he was firm of speech, he could carry the debate. Had it not always been so? But he found he was debating with Mary Martin and himself. He was his own foil. He recognized that it was not a coherent position. He could not reasonably mollify or bargain. There was no pragmatic solution.

"Bear it you must and the sooner you make that decision, the more efficiently we can determine the plans for their transfer, and more important still, explain to them the necessity of the choice. It must be something new and better, an adventure. They must see us in harmony with the choice. There will be a time when, even at their ages, they will have to process grief. It may be even better for them to be here, where their mother will lie buried, than removed from her resting place. There is a comfort in the nearness to the departed. I know. They will have their Aunt Lucinda and their grandfather to help them to process loss.

"You may stay as long as is possible to see that they have what they will need. I will not 'take over' and the arrangements can appear to be yours. There is no need for them to feel you are being separated from them. This can be their home where they have always been happy. You have to go away from time to time and sometimes for long periods, but you will return to them. I will not leave them, ever. They know all the servants. Nothing will be strange."

They passed over the ford at Leaksville and through the small village. The Brougham was a more elegant coach than was common on these streets. Robert waved from his perch at any who would respond. 'People,' thought Stephen. 'Why do I always brighten at the appearance of people. We are a family passing through - no more. Just a family wrapped in grief and I feel the urge to get out and press some hands.'

Each well-meaning phrase from Mary drove like a nail into Stephen's consciousness. He felt like he was being sealed up, shut out. It was not only Martha but he, Stephen A. Douglas, who was being shut away from his own family. "I am resigned, Mary. I probably have been for some little time. Perhaps I had to put up some resistance until we finally reached this place but I knew that once we had, the die would have been cast. I have not previously prepared the boys but also, I have not led them to presume what would happen after their mother's burial. That was selfish, I know, but now we will work together to accommodate their future."

The carriage left the Post Road and turned due south to the Dan ford near Mulberry Island plantation. This was a farm road less intended to be used by fine carriages. It routinely carried men on horseback and farm wagons between fields and more equipment destined to make labor more efficient. The carriage bounced and swayed and Robert had to come down from the driver's seat which

29

caused Stevie to wake. The adult conversation was put away as the destination neared.

Chapter 2

The Settle Cemetery was very near the home of Mary Martin's twin brother, Thomas Settle, so family and friends had retired there after the funeral instead of making the longer trip back to the Martin place. Stevie had been fretful during the grave service, wanting to get down and run around. Robert had been very attentive even crying at one point on seeing that his grandmother and his father had been unable to hold back tears. He was not aware that many of the tears were shed for two motherless little boys.

The setting of the cemetery had maintained the focus on the burial of Martha Martin Douglas, beside her sister and both beside their father. At the Settle home there was a partial metamorphosis into a very formal political gathering. It had not been intended but was inevitable with the presence of so many state and national political leaders. Martha, who had relished her role as wife of the young Senator from Illinois while in Washington, deserved to be honored by politicians at her funeral.

Among the first mourners, after the immediate family, had to be the Governor, David Settle Reid, married to Martha's first cousin. Back in 1843, when Douglas had first taken a seat in Congress it had been the seat next to North Carolina Congressman, David S. Reid. Only three years separated them in age. It had been Reid who had invited Douglass to visit in North Carolina and there to introduce his friend to Martha Martin, daughter of a rich southern plantation owner.

31

The Governor was standing in the parlor that was dusted as appropriate with black crepe over the several portraits and a large gilt mirror. He was retelling the story of the courtship to a circle of about ten people. "Stephen seemed a trifle shy at public gatherings but when we got him into Rockingham County, I guess the languid flow of the Dan River brought peace to his heart. It certainly ripened his heart for, from the moment I introduced him to my beautiful cousin, he was stricken with the most serious onset of love-sickness that it has ever been my opportunity to observe." Smiles and restrained laughter followed. "Uncle Robert had brought Martha to Washington on that first occasion but soon Stephen was making regular visits to North Carolina."

"The 'Little Giant' then rose to the occasion," someone asked irreverently?

"He was of course short, and she was several inches taller but he wore her upon his arm with pleasant satisfaction. I remember observing them once with Douglas' Illinois colleague, Abraham Lincoln and Mary Todd. One could not help notice the variable heights and shapes. Nor could anyone overlook Martha's beauty and Mary Lincoln measured her precisely."

Stephen sat on the central sofa with his sons. He appeared stunned, not altogether assimilating what was going on around him. It was an unaccustomed attitude for on such occasions in other circumstances, he would have been working his way about the room with witty and quotable comments. Periodically each of his friends would glance his way then decide that perhaps the best therapy was a crowded room. He was too numb to participate but he was at home in such a setting.

Calvin Graves from Caswell and Thomas Settle, Senior chatted with some Baptist friends. There were several Trustees of the University of North Carolina about but of the group, these two were also Trustees of the small Baptist College at Wake Forest. Their conversation tended toward the more spiritual initially but soon made the predictable shift to the operation of the plantations along the Dan River.

"I am concluding the documentation to take over "Mulberry Island" from our mutual acquaintance, Alfred Moore Scales. It has made me no friend of that Scales clan but he would have lost the place to his creditors in any event," said Judge Settle.

"I saw his brother, James, at the recent court and there was some bitterness. They will survive. They say Alfred's intention is to take his family south and start again in Mississippi or even in Texas. That state must be filling with depressed land owners from the Carolinas," concluded Graves. "We seem to be experiencing a depopulation of two sorts, failed farmers and slaves from the larger plantations whose owners have purchased estates in the cotton South and are sending them to the cotton fields. The former seems unfortunate but the latter will keep the slave population of North Carolina decreasing and I think that is a good trend."

"It may be a good trend but it does not get us closer to the end of slavery."

33

"It is an advantage in making us less dependent upon our slaves, but I am afraid that slavery is so regional that it cannot be solved by individual states. By pragmatic wisdom or by force, slavery must be finally faced by this republic. It is the termite in our Constitutional government and it the moral blight upon our souls." Settle cast a glance over toward Stephen Douglas. "I respect the efforts of that man while I grieve for him at this moment. He is a national voice of reason. I cannot say that he can broker the solution, but I can tell you that he will be determined in his effort. When I see him in deep conversation with Governor Reid, and my son Thomas, I have hope. You are all Democrats and I am an unreconstructed old Whig but I have hope in your thinking."

"You are kind, Judge, and I do find in our deliberation, the mutual flexibility that should be hopeful in negotiation. We are united in our conviction to preserve the Union but the Union may be the ultimate sacrifice we will all pay if we cannot negotiate an end to slavery soon. Many in the North and the South are prepared to sacrifice Union already, either to end slavery or to preserve it. Both sides would play it like a gold poker chip as a gamble."

"We are dealing with human beings and we cannot be so cavalier that we equate them to poker chips."

"Sorry. Poor choice of metaphor, Judge, but I don't believe I am the one being cavalier."

Thomas Settle, Junior approached his father and Graves. The senior Settle brought him immediately into the conversation demonstrating his unconcealed pride in his young lawyer son. "Calvin, I suppose you know that

Thomas has completed his legal studies at Richmond Pearson's law school in Yadkin. Now there is an old Whig friend who would be right at home in this conversation."

"Hello, Thomas. Congratulations."

"Thomas has taken the position of private secretary to his brother-in-law, the Governor."

"More congratulations!"

"Thank you," said Thomas with a slight bow. "I am very pleased and the prospect of involvement in state government has given me more advancement than I am perhaps worthy of expecting."

"You may be modest in your manner now but I am sure I am not the only person who considers your abilities to be quite bright. Governor Reid would not tolerate less."

this is 1853   he was in Mississippi then moved in 1850

As a contrast to the august atmosphere of this gathering of mourners, Josiah Settle, brother of Thomas Settle and Mary Martin, sat on a straight chair near the wall in the dining room. He had no interest in politics. He was a farmer and successful at his chosen work. It had been Josiah who had encouraged the family to acquire cotton plantations in Alabama and Mississippi touting them as potentially more profitable than their ever-wearing North Carolina tobacco lands.

Josiah's wife had been dead twenty-four years. She was the sister of Thomas' wife, Henrietta Graves. In an awkwardly complicating situation, Josiah had taken a mulatto slave, Nancy Ann, as a common law wife and together they had produced eight children all acknowledged as Josiah's. Nancy Ann was a daughter of Azariah Graves

no!

35

by yet another slave, possibly of his wife's family. So Azariah was the father of Henrietta Settle and Nancy Ann, the slave. Stranger still, she was also the half-sister of Josiah's late wife, Frances Graves. Josiah Settle and his slave wife, as family, were present in the Thomas Settle home. Josiah made it to the dining room but Nancy Ann held back with the servants in order to prevent awkwardness for everyone.

Former Governor Morehead was present. He and his son had ridden over from Leaksville. At a later point he was seen to be colluding with Governor Reid about the slow pace of railroad construction. It seemed such blindness for Legislators in eastern North Carolina to continue to block the north-south railroad through the state just because they wanted the trade through Wilmington. Could they not see that Atlanta was becoming a central transit point for Southern cotton production. Connecting from Richmond to Danville, through central North Carolina to Atlanta had to be the most natural routing and delay only placed the state and the South at an economic disadvantage. "Why, had that road been already built, many more friends from Washington might have been present on this sad occasion. It is just proof that the railroad would in so many ways make our life more dynamic," said Morehead.

Governor Reid found the use of Martha Douglas' funeral as justification for a Piedmont Railroad more political than personally sensitive but he felt comment might appear to be a sever chastisement, so he allowed the remark to pass.

36

Reid's wife, mother of their small son just about the age of Stevie, was attempting to divert the two Douglas boys from the gloom that seemed to cluster around their seated father. "Stephen, let me take the boys to have some sweets in the dining room. Then perhaps they would like to go outside for a while. This room is stuffy with talk."

Douglas looked up as if he had just realized Henrietta was there. "Oh, yes. Thank you, Henrietta. We had such good times together, did we not? Martha was always so much more alive than I was ever to be. She loved to be around people." Steven was blurting out the thoughts that had been circling in his mind. "Take the children, if they will go. Their grandmother has been trying that for some time."

Released from the presence of the children, Douglas became a lure for all the women who had been reserving their hovering instincts. Henrietta Graves, wife of Thomas Settle, senior and mistress of the house, claimed the prime position to Stephen's right. Her daughter-in-law, Mary Glenn Settle appropriated the seat to the left just as swiftly. Others took up seats nearby offering Douglas tea and sweets. He would have preferred a brandy but would not expect it from the gaggle that surrounded him.

"The children, what will you do?" posed one.

"They are so precious, so innocent. To lose a mother at such young ages is a tragedy. They need a woman," was a less than subtle remark.

Stephen cut off such speculation   .
"They will remain here, in North Carolina with their

37

grandmother. It is very painful for me but we have agreed that it best meets their needs and they are familiar with the surroundings here in Rockingham. I may have visualized them as city boys but it seems they will be running barefoot in red clay by summer." He attempted a fragile grin.

Chapter 3

Mary Martin often talked to her grandsons about their mother, even more so as they began to mention her less. She knew that there were times when they yearned for her. More than once she had found Robert crying alone and twice she had found Stevie crying in his bed. She suspected that Robert had said something to bring him to tears but under the circumstances, a scolding seemed inappropriate. She understood that they needed to have a mutual dialogue for the times that they were alone together - the times they were brothers.

The Martin home was not as pretentious a location as had been the home of Robert Martin's uncle, Governor Alexander Martin, called Danbury, very nearby. Many of the finer furnishings were, however, those of the Governor whose younger brother was Mary Martin's late father-in-law. Her husband, Robert, had acquired the old Danbury plantation and Mount Pleasant adjoining, that had been Pleasant Henderson's place. So here, along the south side of the Dan River, Mary Martin owned more than a mile's worth of tobacco plantations.

Judge Settle made every effort to spend long days at the Martin Plantation. Sometimes it was to assist Mary with her overseers in the management of the land. Others he spent more with the boys. He was mildly concerned that on most days they played outside with some of the slave children. It was satisfying to see them play so innocently but there was also overhanging caution. What were they learning and how and how were their attitudes being

Martha Martin Douglas (1829-1853)

shaped? Only once had he thought to himself, how are those little black children being affected? Considering the pre-ordained status of their lives, how does such interaction impact them? Then he turned back to concentrate on his nephew's interests.

The boys had enjoyed the single visit they had from their father before he returned to Washington but they did not ignore the sadness in his speech or his actions. They laughed a little extra around him but he hardly responded. They had to suggest activities as if they were trying to improve his spirits. Of course they were not aware of the opportunities all during the day, when he would slip a bottle from his pocket and take a swig of his brandy. Mary saw it and tried subtle ways of chastisement.

His plan to make a trip to Europe in May, startled Mary but the boys did not understand his intent. "I will be visiting all the great states of Europe, boys."

"What is Europe," asked Stevie?

"Be still," said Robert harshly, as if he understood so much better.

"Countries are like states in America. You both remember when we lived in Illinois and of course you remember Washington. Well, across the Atlantic Ocean there is an area known as Europe that is similarly divided but not into states. They call themselves countries."

"Is Mr. Pierce their President," asked Stevie attempting to indicate that he had been following all his father's earlier attempts to give him some information.

Again Robert cut in with a tone of disgust. "No Stevie. Mr. Pierce is President of the United States. In Europe they have Kings and things."

Douglas chuckled. "Yes they do. They have 'Kings and things.'"

"Will you be seeing the Kings papa? You are a Senator and that is almost the same as being a King," said Robert.

"You give me too much importance son. I do hope that I will be able to meet some heads of state and I will be interested in seeing how their individual governments work."

"You just said they don't have states, Papa. Why do they have heads of states?" Stevie thought he had found a very wise contradiction.

"Just a term, boy, just a term. Means about the same thing." Douglas had not even tried to deal with his son's concern. Did he not have time for being a father?

Mary Martin was observing and she thought later that this was a first sign that Douglas was prepared to put his sons out of his way so that he could get on with himself.

Mary made a special trip of excitement out of the planned excursion with her grandsons to the Settle cemetery in mid-summer. "It will be like a picnic," she announced. "We will be going to visit your Mother."

The boys were puzzled by the prospect. Of course, they knew they were not going to see their mother, although Stevie somehow hoped that they might. Then their

42

grandmother confused them further by saying they would also be seeing Aunt Lucinda and their grandfather.

The day itself co-operated. The sky was blue and except far to the west, it was cloudless. As they passed by the courthouse in Wentworth, Mary was conscious that the Martin chaise was a bit thread bear, needing a general refinishing and new upholstery. Her husband had never arranged it so Mary felt no need to spend the money. Anyway, she knew of no one nearby who could do justice to such expensive equipage.

They stopped briefly at Wright Tavern for some tea and cakes and to let the boys run and the horses rest. On the road again, they had less than two hours before they approached the cemetery down a slight grade. Hon was the driver and Billy Jesse was acting as a footman. They were able to pull off the road and Billy Jesse handed each child and then Mary, down from the carriage. Hon lifted a large whicker hamper down from the roof to Billy Jesse. "Its heavy," he said unnecessarily.

The boys each took one of Mary's hands appearing to help her up the hill. Actually each was feeling a certain security holding hands with their grandmother. Robert was the first to see what looked like three white boxes all in a row. "I see them," announced Robert.

"Yes, there they are."

"Is Mama in one of those boxes, grandma," wondered Stevie.

"No. No, child. Let us get there and we can sit down and rest and I will help you understand."

l to r:Mary Martin, Martha Martin Douglas, Lucinda Martin, Robert Martin

The hillside had been cleared some years before by the slaves - trees cut and stumps removed and burned. The surrounding area was wooded and the huge virgin oaks and chestnuts gave shade to the open summit. There was a path leading up from the road that wound slightly to make the grade more gradual. There were a few marked graves scattered about but now the three boxes of marble side-by-side dominated the site.

In the hamper were three folding stools and when Hon had brought them out, Mary and the boys sat down. It was a peaceful setting - open yet shaded. Mary knew that for the first time, the three tomb markers would all be in place, but she was not quite prepared for the impact the

44

sight now had on her. She rested for a moment then directed the slaves to spread the small table from the hamper but to leave the food in place for the time being. Then she got up and walked slowly over to the nearest marble box where she placed her hand.

"This is the grave of your grandfather. You remember him don't you boys?

"Yes, ma'am."

Then she got the angle of the light just right and read to the boys, "Robert Martin, born 12 April 1781 in Rockingham County, NC, died 25 May 1848." Except for a soft chorus of birds, everything was still. The boys watched their grandmother for some sign of what they should do or say. She seemed suspended in her thoughts.

"Was grandpa old?" wondered Stevie.

"No," said his grandmother, "never to me. You know Stevie that he was born just after we had that great battle at Guilford Courthouse in the Revolutionary War." She knew the boys liked to hear the tall tales of the Revolution. "His mother was a Drennen and lived up in Hunterdon County in New Jersey. She and your great grandpa were not married. He was already living over at the Danbury house with his mother but the family had all come down from New Jersey just as the Revolution began and the boys often went back up there on business. I think that Robert was a young scoundrel and he carried on some 'monkey business' with Miss Drennen and before he was through, he had a son and daughter but they were never married. Those children were brought down here and Robert benefited greatly by the success of his older

45

siblings. His son, your grandfather, right here," she patted the granite, "had an agile mind. When he came courting, I knew that he was a fine prize and I wasted no effort in hooking him in."

"You mean like a fish, grandma," wondered Stevie?

"I bet he thought he was a fish, Stevie."

"Why are they in boxes, grandma," wondered Robert?

"They look like boxes, don't they, but they are marble, four sides and a flat top. It is a style of monument that is popular at the moment. Grandpa and I agreed upon it before he died and we have used it for Lucinda and Martha as they died. I suppose they will be the same for me. They are each buried in the ground and the boxes just stand on the ground above them."

Robert and Steven accepted the explanation silently unsatisfied in the knowledge that had been shared.

Mary moved to the middle box. "This is your Aunt Lucinda. You never saw her because she died before your parents met. Again Mary read aloud, the inscription. "Lucinda Settle Martin, daughter of Robert and Mary Martin, died 15 September 1846." Mary was now tearful.

"Was she pretty, grandma," asked Robert anxious to cheer his grandmother from her thoughts.

"Oh, very," she said. "She was just about to be married when she became suddenly ill and was gone in a day." Mary talked for some time about the beauty and promise of Lucinda.

"She died before grandpa, didn't she?"

"Yes. I really believe that he never recovered from the shock of her death. That sometimes happens to people. They are so overcome with their grief, that they can never again right the ship and balance their lives."

"Will that happen to Papa," wondered Robert.

Stephen's head popped up for the answer having never thought about the question before.

"No indeed, boys. Your father is strong and he has important work to do and there is so much expected of him that he would consider himself a coward to give up."

Mary moved over to her daughter, Martha. "This is your mother." It sounded so strange. A box was what they saw but a grandmother saying, "This is your Mother. The stone was brought by your father from Washington with your mother's casket. It was only put in place last week and the four small cedar trees were planted at each corner. I wanted to see it and I wanted you to see it." She waited for a response from either of the boys. Nothing.

"Your father wanted these words. "Here lies Martha Martin, wife of Stephen A. Douglas of Ill., died Washington, DC 19 January 1853, in the 25th year of her age."

Still there were no words from the boys. Then Robert reached out and touched the lip of the tablet stone. "It is so white," he said as a spoken thought. "Like she is just there." Then he pointed to one of the small cedars a few feet from each corner of the tomb. "Why did Papa want to put the trees like that?

"Cedars are sometimes considered a symbol of grief, Robert. One day they will be tall and, like the 'marble box' they will mark her grave."

"Grandma, what does grief mean? People keep talking about grief and I know it has something to do with Mama dying but I can't quite figure why."

Mary paused a moment. "Robert, you know how you and Stevie sometimes get sad when you think about your Mama. There are times when you particularly want her with you. Well, that is grief - when we are sad."

"Then this is a place of grief, isn't it?"

"In some ways, yes. Don't be afraid of grief. It is natural sometimes to be sad and to grieve. We have lost something. But we have memory to connect us to those we love who have gone away. Grief and memory work together to keep Mama, and Lucinda, and Grandpa with us, in our hearts and heads. Your Mama will always be a part of your lives now and forever." She was watching Stevie, knowing she was talking to Robert and hoping that in some way her words were understood by the younger boy.

"I want you boys to feel that this is a special place for you. Right now, that is a strange thing for you because all you see is this sparkling white box. It only represents your mother. Her soul is in heaven with Jesus but her body is here. I remember when she was just a little girl and we lived over at the Danbury House of your great Uncle Alexander Martin. A Baptist Preacher named Elias Dodson came and Martha was saved and became a believer. She believed in Jesus and now she is with him in Heaven."

Robert Martin Douglas-Stephen A. Douglas, Jr. ca 1860

Childhood photo-Robert Martin Douglas (Courtesy Mrs. Lucy Blum)

49

Robert looked up and commented seriously, "That is hard for me to understand. She is here under this box and I know it is just her body, but she is in Heaven with Jesus. I know you say it is just her soul but I have never seen a soul."

"Don't worry, boys. One day it will be clearer to you. That will be part of your growing up. For now just be certain that your Mother is at peace.

"All your lives you will be able to return again to this place and be near to her. You lost her when you were so young but she does not have to seem far away from you. Don't be afraid of this place. We will come whenever you like. Will you share her with me? She is my little girl you know."

"Grandma. Why did she go away," asked Steven clearly seeking a clarifying answer to many unasked questions.

"Because God wanted her, Stevie. She was needed."
"I want her too, grandma."

"I know that you do, so you will have to try very hard to remember her in your heart because that is where you have her."

First Steven and then Robert, wrapped their arms around the billowing skirt of their grandmother. Then quickly, as if to say 'all right, that's over,' Stephen pointed to a large square depression just beyond his mother's grave. "What's that hole for?"

Mary gathered her whit around her. "Oh, that is something I wanted to explain to you. Several years before you grandfather died, he had already bought all of the land of your great uncle, Governor Alexander Martin. You remember we have talked about him before. He was elected Governor many times and he helped write the Constitution of the United States. Well, when he died his body was placed in what was called a stone crypt in a high bank above Dan River at his Danbury Plantation. And only four days later the Governor's mother, your great, great grandmother, died. She was old and she grieved for her son and she was buried in that crypt. A few years later, when your great grandfather, Robert, died, he was also buried in what they called the family crypt."

The boys were studying the spot intently as if they could somehow see this 'cloud of witnesses.' "Some years passed and when your grandfather bought Danbury, it became his family responsibility to keep up the crypt. By then it had become very weakened by trees that had uprooted and water that had washed into the cut in the hillside. He decided that he must move the graves to protect them and so he had to choose a place. We had already buried Lucinda here and Robert knew that when he died, he would be buried here also, so he brought all three bodies here and buried them together in that spot. He always intended to mark them properly but never got around to it. I guess it will be up to you one day to put up a marker."

"OK," said Stephen as if he had just sealed a deal and he was off to other locations in the cemetery. There were not really many stones.

"Who are they," asked Robert pointing to two graves together.

"They are my mother and father. She died just a year ago but you were in Washington. Over there is my brother Benjamin."

"And this one over near grandpa?"

"That is your Aunt Francis, the wife of my brother Josiah."

"You mean Uncle Josiah who has the slave wife and all those slave children?"

Mary couldn't hold back now. The boys had obviously overheard the family gossip and if they had never asked before, here was a grave that brought up the subject. "Yes, this was Uncle Josiah's first wife and she had a half-sister and that is the mother of his children now."

The answer obviously begged again for more questions but for the moment the children were satisfied with what they had heard. Almost immediately, they bounced over to another very white marble stone. It was upright and stood about fifty feet from the nearest other stone.

"Whose is this? It says 'Washington' like where we lived," said Robert, as if he had a true discovery.

"That is a slave boy named Washington. He was the first son of Uncle Josiah and Nancy Ann and he accidentally shot himself on Christmas day in 1846."

Mary was prepared for the next question which came from Robert but was a single thought of both boys. "Why did he shot himself, Grandma?"

"He did not intend to. He had been sent to pick up some birds the men had shot but he forgot he was carrying a gun that he did not know was loaded. When his father called him back, somehow he tripped and fell and the gun went off, killing him. He was just sixteen and he was hurrying to please the hunters who had just flushed a large covey of quail. It was a very sad time. All the family and all the slaves mourned together and his daddy put up that stone after they buried him here with the family."

The boys could see that he was not exactly located 'with the family' but did not question.

Chapter 4

Senator Douglas returned from Europe in October and immediately was immersed in national politics. His negotiation of the Compromise of 1850, which had made his political position so strong, had also brought a prospect of a long term easing of the slavery question. By 1854, the issue was again before the legislature with the need for territorial organization of Kansas and Nebraska . The territories were above the 36° 30' line where the Missouri Compromise had prohibited slavery. Douglas now had to compromise his opposition on slavery in order to get the transcontinental railroad to California to accept the so-called northern route through Chicago. At first vilified by Abolitionists, he was able to use the will of the voter as an acceptable justification for his compromise. His 'principled argument' espoused popular sovereignty of allowing the people of a territory to decide whether to permit or exclude slavery.

There was then little public awareness that in 1847, that the day after Douglas' marriage to Martha Martin, Robert Martin had handed Douglas a sealed package of papers. Inside Douglas found a deed to all Martin's land and slaves at the Pearl River in Lawrence County, Mississippi.

"I cannot accept," said Douglas immediately, seeming to be startled by the prospect. "I am no Abolitionist, and I have no sympathy with them in their wild schemes and ultra views respecting slavery, but I am a northern man by birth, education, and residence, and am totally ignorant of such plantations and the manner in which they should be governed. I am wholly incompetent to such a task." Martin was also surprised because he assumed that his prospective son-in-law was well versed on the extensive estate that would come to Martha, the older man's lone surviving daughter.

Senator Stephen A. Douglas of Illinois

"I thought that you knew full well the extent of my estate and that in marrying my daughter you were certainly due to come into this inheritance at my death."

Douglas was risking an insult to his future father-in-law who knew full well the fame of Douglas as an astute attorney and political operative. He was maneuvering to

find a position from which he could get his cake and eat it at the same time. He could not long pretend to be
either humbled or surprised. Robert Martin knew his law as well and they would hammer out the quid pro quo of any political compromise. Douglas, who had himself been turned down by Mary Todd, some time before, had the much improved prospects of being very wealthy and being politically powerful, with a beautiful wife thrown in.

Sen. Stephen A. Douglas lying in state

"The dilemma is slavery and we must look to the future to model the solution," said Martin. "Martha is my daughter and it should be hoped you and she will have children and heirs. Whatever the source of my worth, if God concurs, it should devise to them. How do we accomplish that while preserving your position with the body politic? Is that our consideration?"

Douglas admired the insightfulness of the elder man and while guarding his interests, he deferred to him. "I see that you are well advised and we share the purpose."

"Martha's mother should first be provided for during the remainder of her life," suggested Martin as an opener, "in surroundings to which she is accustomed. She should have the home place, the slaves, $200 yearly from my stock in the Bank of the State of North Carolina, and $200 yearly from the yield of all my property."

Details of the sale of various individual tracts would be handled by Douglas with assistance of Martin's nephew, Governor David Settle Reid. "The pair of you will be able to administer the estate from here and from Washington." There was land in New Orleans and New York to be sold by agents.

"Here is the rub now, Stephen - the land on the Pearl River in Mississippi. We cannot pretend that this is not my most lucrative property. It is a southern cotton plantation, very rich, and productive only because of about a hundred slaves I have there with another thirty on the road.

"Could you be politically viable if, as manager of the Mississippi plantation, you were paid out of the proceeds of a plantation owned by your wife? You can truly claim that you do not own slaves, even that you are opposed to the ownership of slaves. It will be disingenuous, I know, but true in the law."

Douglas did not immediately answer. "I am not so transparent that I do not understand much of the political struggle over slavery as disingenuous. Politics and morality are often more appearance than reality and they need only a little evidence to prove credibility. It may be difficult for me to purport that profits from a cotton plantation do not come from the backs of slaves. In debate, however, it is possible to parry such an assertion as an insult to ones ethical integrity. After all the value of management may be much in perception and who outside the arrangement can pretend to know that value." Douglas was voicing the musings of his political machinations.

Robert Martin smiled. "One further demand," he posited. "If my daughter should die without issue, it is my wish that sufficient money should be taken out of the last crop to equip and to transport my slaves in Mississippi to Liberia."

Douglas recognized the subtle call of his hand. Martin's face was impassive. Having rejected his slaves as an openhanded gift, Martin intended to be certain that Douglas would not have them by surviving his daughter.

SETTLE – GRAVES -- DOUGLAS

Josiah Settle = Elizabeth Allen

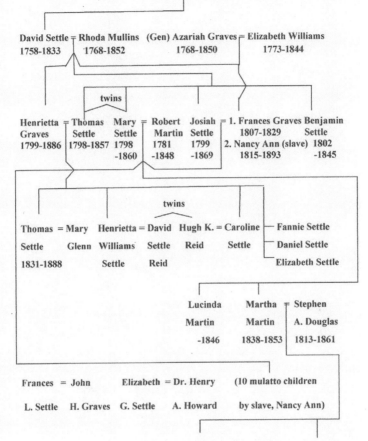

David Settle = Rhoda Mullins (Gen) Azariah Graves = Elizabeth Williams
1758-1833   1768-1852   1768-1850   1773-1844

twins

Henrietta = Thomas   Mary = Robert   Josiah = 1. Frances Graves   Benjamin
Graves   Settle   Settle Martin   Settle   1807-1829   Settle
1799-1886 1798-1857 1798   1781   1799   2. Nancy Ann (slave) 1802
                     -1860   -1848   -1869   1815-1893   -1845

twins

Thomas = Mary   Henrietta = David   Hugh K. = Caroline   — Fannie Settle
Settle   Glenn Williams   Settle   Reid   Settle   — Daniel Settle
1831-1888   Settle   Reid   Elizabeth Settle

Lucinda   Martha = Stephen
Martin   Martin   A. Douglas
-1846   1838-1853 1813-1861

Frances = John   Elizabeth = Dr. Henry   (10 mulatto children
L. Settle H. Graves G. Settle   A. Howard   by slave, Nancy Ann)

Robert = Jesse M. Dick   Stephen A.

59

Chapter 5

Robert Martin executed his will in November 1847 six months after his daughter's wedding. In another six months, he was dead. The Douglas' moved from Springfield to Chicago to the shores of Lake Michigan. Stephen made trips to Mississippi, without fanfare, to secure his management responsibilities. Martha's son, Robert Martin, was born in 1849 and named for his late grandfather, and Steven, Junior. was born almost two years later. Although this was a productive period in Douglas' political life, he took his family on regular visits to North Carolina to see Martha's widowed mother. Mary had a remarkably powerful pair of executors to manage her estate in Senator Douglas and her nephew, David Settle Reid.

The devastation of Martha Martin Douglas' early death as the result of childbirth, enervating to her husband, gave to her mother, the care of the two boys. They became Mary's boys. Mary had seen quite properly, that their father was so personally ambitious that the tragedy of his wife's death would either emotionally break him or drive his aspirations at the expense even of his children. She gave them security and a familiar environment and probably, denying it even to herself, she sought to become their surrogate mother   .

Robert and Stephen were periodically in Washington with their father but when there, they were really under the care of Douglas' sister and brother-in-law whom Douglas had installed in his house at the time of his

European trip. Julius and Sarah Granger assumed a special custodial function in this family arrangement. They saw the loss of his partner as so devastating to Douglas that they feared for his life and sanity. Martha's memory became precious as did the interests of her sons. With Mary Martin, they developed a common paternal practice to undergird the children in the absence of their father.

Douglas, released from his responsibility to his children, and driven by his political motivation, was introduced in Washington society to Adele Cutts, great niece of former President James Madison and Dolly Madison. A small inconvenience was that she was Catholic. It was 1857. Martha Douglas had been a sweet, demure, loving mother who referred to her husband always as 'Judge Douglas.' Adele Cutts was also beautiful but very accustomed to the demands of society in the national capital. She was the mature partner for Douglas' ambitions. She intended to rehabilitate his image. She stopped his drinking and converted his rather slovenly and disinterested concern for his appearance into the well manicured statesman he had previously been. Before the wedding, Douglas had packed up Martha's portrait and the one of Martha's father, "and certain articles of silver," and entrusted them to his sister to keep, "until the children were grown up."

Mary Martin received news of Stephen's remarriage with misgivings. She had been uneasy about the carelessness with which he seemed to have been plying his personal life but that only seemed to have been making secure her position as related to his sons. By spring, however, she had parted with them as they left by coach for Washington, half hoping that there might be a prospect they would find a normal family life again. Julius Granger waited a few months later, to inform Mary Martin, "of the health of Dear little Robert and Stevie, who started yesterday for Chicago with Judge Douglas & lady." He became more ominous, "to say that the Judges wife is very jealous of any other persons love to the boys."

Then a promised note came from little Robert in Chicago saying, "I am very happy here with Father and Mother." Mary was certain that Adele Cutts was easing her aside as she appropriated her step children into her image of the Senator's proper family. Adele was astute to her concern and heading off any rupture, invited Mary to Washington for a visit. That did not go well and Mary departed for her return prematurely. The Grangers arrived to find her gone and "were mortified."

Adele was pregnant and perhaps she did not want the mother of Douglas' first wife there to attend her. The baby was premature and lived only a few hours. Adele nearly died also. She would undergo one more unsuccessful pregnancy but she had to settle on the cast that she would present to the electorate as Senator Douglas' wholesome family.

Mary Martin died in the summer of 1860. She divided her dower between her two grandsons but to Robert Martin Douglas alone, she left the Dan River plantation.

The Mississippi plantation became part of the flotsam created by the Civil War and the end of slavery. As heirs of their mother, Robert and Stevie held title with

Dan River plantation home of Robert and Mary Settle Martin west of Wentworth. The house was demolished in the mid-1930s.

Courtesy *The State Magazine* September 20, 1941.

"Mount Julep," the Washington residence of Stephen A. and Martha Martin Douglas, which was purchased in April 1851.

Courtesy of Mrs. Lucile Reid Fagg.

their father as guardian. They were twelve and ten respectively. About the time of his second marriage, Douglas found land, more productive than the Lawrence County land, in Washington County on the Mississippi River - one of the Bayou counties. The courts approved his petition to sell the first plantation, as guardian, in three parcels and to transfer the one hundred and forty-eight slaves to the second plantation.

Douglas' campaign for the Presidency failed and Lincoln's election was followed by the outbreak of the war. Senator Douglas died June 3, 1861 and on January 1, 1863, Lincoln issued the Emancipation Proclamation freeing the slaves in the southern states.

Adele Cutts, now the widow Douglas, raised her stepsons as Catholics in her Washington home.

In 1872, both having reached their majority, Robert and Stephen Douglas brought three separate suits in Lawrence County, Mississippi for ejectment against James W. Bennett and James Strictland, John Gartman, and Peter C. Quinn for recovery claiming they had not been paid for the sale of the Mississippi land. Gartman compromised.

The case turned on the right of the court at the time to have agreed to the appointment of Senator Douglas as guardian for his sons. Douglas had been paid in that capacity for the land in Lawrence and had not reported it to the record. The court made excuse for the deceased Senator presuming he was then embroiled in the Presidential campaign and that his sons might assume that payment was due him in his capacity as manager.

The case also ignored the fact that two years after his death, the one hundred forty-five slaves that Senator Douglas never owned but managed, were freed by Lincoln and subsequently by the Fourteenth Amendment to the Constitution ending slavery. Many of those slaves had their roots in North Carolina at the old Martin plantation on the Dan. Their lives floated beneath the surface of this public story about the 'Little Giant."

BOOK III
WASHINGTON A SLAVE

Chapter 1

The success of the "Big Sweep" for 2008 was demonstrated by the trucks filled with trash that lined the road. Eli was walking by and stopped suddenly as he passed the bed of a blue truck at a filling station and looked more closely. Marble is starkly white even if it is aged. Someone who has for years had an interest in history of the built environment, old houses, cemeteries, Indian relics, knows the sight of marble. Eli reached up on the truck and pushed back a bundle of tires, limbs and cans from the small white piece of visible stone and saw what he had expected, a full tombstone, 20" wide and perhaps 35" tall. It was what he saw next inscribed on the surface that made his heart leap.

"To the memory of WASHINGTON
A good servant of J. Settle
Who accidentally shot himself
Christmas Day 1846
16th year of his age."

Eli remembered this stone and he recalled the several discussions that he had during recent years peculating about its disappearance from the Settle Cemetery off Brooks Road. Many members of the Rockingham County Historical Society had bemoaned the theft of this particular stone because it had this inscription and because it was the only grave in Rockingham County of a slave marked with a manufactured stone, and in such a particular way.

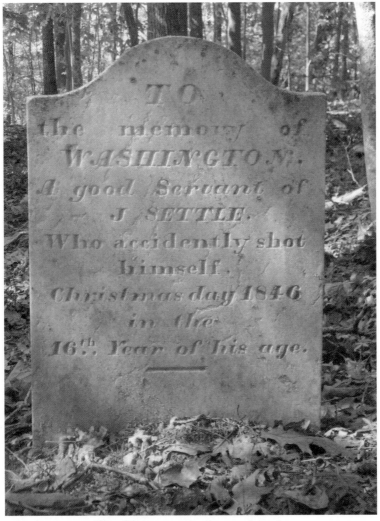

Washington stone as replaced

When confronting a tombstone thief, it is best to be circumspect. He simply asked casually "where did you come by this?" Eli had struck an embarrassing nerve.

"Oh, that? Found it a few years ago sitting by the side of the road somewhere out in the county. Thought today might be a good time to get rid of it. I can't use it."

"Wouldn't have been near Brooks Road, would it?"

"No! No! May have been over near Eden. Don't really remember."

"I know where it came from and I'd like to take it back. Would you mind?"

"No. You go ahead. If I'd known where it came from, I'd have taken it back. Just don't tell nobody where you found it."

A few months later with some members of the Historical Society, Eli carried the marble slab back to Settle Cemetery. They relocated it as close to the place their collective memories thought it had stood. The bottom had been broken off so when back in place, it stood up lower than any had remembered but, by miracle, it was back.

Washington's tombstone told a haunting story evoking obvious sorrow over a sudden, antebellum hunting accident. 'All you who pass by read my tragic story,' it seemed to plead.

For many years, people did read it but no one was fully satisfied that this abbreviated report of tragedy told the full story.

On the other side of the cemetery knoll was another grave. This one was for "Frances, wife of Josiah Settle, 2

April 1807 - 7 October 1829, in 23rd year." She was Frances Lea Graves, daughter of Azariah Graves of Caswell County. She had married the brother of the twins, Mary Settle Martin and Thomas Settle, a US Congressman and Speaker of the North Carolina House of Commons. Josiah was a good farmer and already he had acquired considerable land and numbers of slaves. His marriage to Frances, however, was sadly brief.

After that Josiah chose to do what many southern plantation owners did. He 'took up with' one of his slaves. Not just any one but Nancy Ann who happened to be half sister of Frances Graves - another of Azariah's daughters but by a slave from the Williams plantation.

"J. Settle," was Josiah Settle who placed this marble stone to his first child by his mulatto slave, Nancy Ann.

BOOK IV
MY INTENDED WIFE AND CHILDREN

Chapter 1

Josiah Settle was as unconventional within the Settle family as he was a challenge to the public structure of the institution of slavery. He was the brother of old Judge Tom Settle, and he had sat taciturn beside the wall at the wake for Martha Martin Douglas, while his mulatto concubine remained in the kitchen. He had not only produced nine children by Nancy Graves, but he had two grown daughters by his first wife, Frances Lea Graves.

Frances Graves was the daughter of Brigadier General Azariah Graves of Caswell County. The Graves and Settle families were both staunch Baptists. Azariah was commander of the 16th Brigade, 3rd Division of the North Carolina Militia during the War of 1812. His wife, Elizabeth "Betsy" Williams. was the daughter of John Williams, a Colonel in the Revolutionary War. The union was of two of the important plantation families of Caswell and Rockingham Counties.

Frances' older sister, Henrietta Graves, was the wife of Thomas Settle. So in 1820, Thomas Settle had married Azariah Graves' daughter, Henrietta and in 1824, Thomas' brother, Josiah, had married Azariah's other daughter, Frances Graves. Understanding the relationship in these marriages is critical in setting up the social impact of the choices that were to be made within a few years.

Josiah and Frances lived in the plantation house built by his parents, David and Rhoda Settle. In a few years, when David died, Josiah would inherit the home plantation and maintain his mother for the remainder of her

But 1840 cens [illegible handwritten note]

life. The two story frame house sat near Jones Branch of Lower Hogan's Creek. Its federal style gave it character beyond the usual log farmhouses of the neighbors but it could not be considered as one of the finer antebellum plantations of a somewhat later period. For the Settles, it was still the 'home house.'

Josiah Settle had acquired considerable wealth as a slave trader. He was active in buying slaves from Africa until that commerce was effectively curtailed by the British Navy. Still, the domestic market remained strong and he sold slaves throughout the lower South. His activity as a slave trader makes all his actions in his later life seem either contradictory or shows a significant capacity for ambivalence.

In Caswell County, Azariah Graves had a relationship with a slave who might have been brought to his marriage as part of his wife's inheritance. This single example demonstrates how common was this practice, which constituted rape, of a master on a slave woman within the plantation society. Although she may have acquiesced, she had no recourse, no way to appeal, and nowhere to go. The act was, therefore, a prima fascia violation of her personhood. Since the child of a slave woman was automatically a slave, which constituted the certainty of black blood, the only routine way of suggesting the white patriarchal relationship, was the identification in the public record of the child as a mulatto. Azariah Graves at the time had 38 slaves which was a typical holding for a North Carolina Piedmont plantation.

Josiah and his wife, Frances, had two daughters, Elizabeth in 1827 and Frances in 1829 when Frances, the mother, had died in childbirth. The slave, Nancy Ann, fathered by Azariah Graves (or certainly a member of his

JOSIAH SETTLE – Mixed Family

(Gen) Azariah Graves = Elizabeth Williams   David Settle = Rhoda Mullins
Mullins

Francis Lea = Josiah Settle = Nancy Ann   Thomas Settle = Henrietta
Graves   Graves (Mulatto)   Graves

(All NC) – (All Mulatto)

Washington	Sidney	Robert = Elizabeth	Henry = Molly	William = Josephine
1830-1846	1832-	Pinckney Weaver	Clay Berry	Harrison Scott
Killed				
Accidentally		1834- 1864-1903	1838-	1840-

(Tishomingo Co. MS)

Winfield = Eliza	Matilda	Cornelia = James	Josiah = 1.Theresa T.
Scott Alberson	1841	1846 Townsend	Thomas Vogelsang
Francine			1850-1915 2. Frances
			McCullough

Josephine   William E.
1852   Reynolds

76

family) had been given to Frances, her half sister. So the two Settle sons had married the two Graves sisters and their half-sister, the mulatto daughter of their father, was a slave of one of those daughters.

The family embarrassment goes further. A year after Frances' death, Josiah Settle produced a mulatto son, Washington, by this slave, Nancy Ann.

"Have you lost all principles of good manners, Josiah," Thomas Settle asked his brother? "It is embarrassing enough that Father Graves sired this woman by his slave. We thought that bringing her from Caswell to Rockingham would at least remove the obvious from gossip. Now, you have taken to bed this woman and produced a mulatto son. It has become appalling."

"Did Henrietta send you with this message?" Josiah demanded. "Will this be embarrassing to you politically or personally? You see, Thomas, I am just a farmer. I do not have to protect my political future and I am surely not responsible for protecting yours. Frances was dear to me and I was true to her in our marriage."

"That at least is re-assuring."

"Now, like you, Thomas, I have a son. Be happy for me. I was so proud I named him Washington."

"Don't be trivial. What you have done is an abomination. You cannot be held in respect when you rape your own slaves. Think of the human insensitivity. In the South, we are saddled by the sin of slavery. To compound that sin by rape, is unthinkable."

Thomas Settle, Sr. (1798-1857)

Henrietta Graves Settle (1799-1886)

"Too far, Thomas! Too far! I have been a slave trader but I am now as opposed to slavery as are you but I am not hypocritical about it. I see no error when my relationship is consensual and that is between me and Nancy. You and the rest of your plantation elite can make any assumptions that you wish. The law prevents us from being married but it does nothing to prevent us from enjoying the fruits of our relationship. I am satisfied that Nancy Ann does not consider herself to be abused or taken advantage of, nor does she derive any advantage within the slave community."

"If you believe that, Josiah, you are a fool. Your slaves, and mine, and everyone else's are fully aware of what goes on in the big house. Do you take her to bed there or do you go to her in the quarters?"

"Why don't you ask your slaves if they all know so much?"

Thomas shifted his approach. "What can possibly be our relationship within the family? Azariah at least had the good sense to find his pleasure outside the family and consider he had produced another hand. You have produced a bastard!"

"Do you charge me with being something other than most slave owners of our like because Nancy Ann is you sister-in-law? You see, there is the rub. My relationship must play out on the matrix of slavery with all its protections, and peculiar laws, and religious contradictions. Thomas, we are all playing upon that matrix and we are all lesser for it. I am content. I do not intend to apologize or to send Nancy Ann off. As long as she consents, I will lie with her. We will have other children. I will treat them as I treat my own two daughters but I will not force an unnatural relationship upon them because of the system for which they have no responsibility."

"You mean to be 'one happy family!' That is a mirage and you know it."

"No mirage. I will live with my daughters, in the house. Nancy Ann will live with her children in her quarters. We will all come and go as we please."

"Will your children be field hands?"

"I will educate my children, those by Frances and those by Nancy Ann. When the time comes I will free Nancy and my children and they will become what they seek to become."

"Oh, Josiah, you are such a blind fool. This path you set out is not open to us, legally or practically. There can be no happiness when a man's family is the source of his sorrow."

"I will be the one to live with the consequences."

Josiah had a similar confrontation with his parents. "I have a son born of Nancy Ann," he announced to his stunned parents. "We call him, Washington."

Neither parent spoke nor did they display any outward shock. David Settle was seventy-three. His activity was restricted but he was the Settle patriarch.

Finally he began, "I have been proud of the lives of my children. They have all built well on top of what I have been able to provide. I cannot deny you the choice that you have made, Josiah, but it is also impossible for me to condone it. You are an adult and no decision you can ever make will disappoint me. The line may be fine but the choice is yours."

Rhoda seemed eager to add, "What about your daughters, Josiah. They are such sweet little girls and they are left motherless. Don't they require your first thoughts?"

"Frances and Elizabeth will always have my love and attention. They will also benefit from two large and closely associated families. They will not want for either support or love."

"Nancy Ann is your slave, Josiah. The law covers your actions but we have always taught you that you were responsible to God's law."

"Father, I had a similar conversation with Thomas. I told him that I was content with my actions. They were made upon rules of social appropriateness that we all know to be hypocritical. By that I do not mean to find an excuse but to say only that I will absorb the consequences. I am sorry that the results of my actions cannot be limited to me but affect my entire family. I can only ask for your tolerance."

Chapter 2

In this environment, a white master producing a child with a slave was so commonplace that white society did not imagine it as rape. It was simpler to convince oneself that a slave would certainly be pleased to produce a child by the master, considering it to be some kind of special favor. Had Josiah simply kept his slave mistress quiet in the quarters, his actions would not have been anything more than routine. Slave owners could joke about their own or their neighbor's contribution to the increase of their slave colony. The course that Josiah took was more nuanced because along with other members of his family, he considered slavery as an abomination. His action attempted to break the hold of slavery, not by becoming an Abolitionist and freeing his slaves, but by living within the practice of slavery and operating against its hypocrisy. This is not the case of taking a middle ground but of trying to have it both ways, leaving the heavy lifting to others. Ultimately, Josiah created what must seem his own hypocrisy.

"They have been informed," Josiah said to Nancy Ann when he came to her a few hours later in the quarters. "I told Thomas first and asked him to tell Benjamin and Mary. Then I told my parents." He paused. "They all knew you were with child but the shock was my acknowledgement that the child was mine and I was pleased. They know now. They will have to make their own peace with their prejudice."

"Josiah, you said you were pleased. Are you, pleased, Josiah?

"Yes Nancy. The child is equally ours. He is our son and I will always treat him as such."

Nancy's head bowed to the small child, the bundle wrapped at her breast. "He is ours," she said aloud but mostly to herself.

"Our relationship, Nancy, will always exist as part of the circumstances of where we live. The law says you are legally a slave and that a child born of a slave mother is automatically a slave. We are all human beings and the law cannot dictate how we relate to each other as human beings. By that definition, we will always live in two realities. We will have to become accustomed to that accommodation and the hurt that it implies. We must always remember that our true reality is as human beings, as a human family. We may have other children. We may seek to move our place of residence if we think we can improve the circumstances of life for either one of us or our children. We will hope for a level of support from our families and friends but we cannot depend on that. If it comes to us, it will be an extra blessing. This is a difficult path but it is not impossible."

Josiah found himself unable to speak of love or intimacy. Strange. He knew both to be part of his marriage to Frances but they were not words he could use as he talked now with Nancy. He knew it was a fault. He felt guilt.

Nancy too recognized that though his words had been comforting and re-assuring, they had not spoken of

love and certainly the word marriage had not been coupled when he mentioned the human family. For the first time it came to her that she would have to be satisfied with what she had and what Josiah had been willing to say. He was still her master. What he had offered to her, had made her more than a slave but not a wife or lover.

Josiah continued to live in the big house in the room he had occupied with Frances. Nancy and Washington lived in her quarters. Some evenings he came to her and on a few occasions, she was able to come to him in the master's house. Since Nancy was a house servant, she did much of her work around the big house, coming and going at will. It was rare that she experienced any subtle change in her dealings with David and Rhoda Settle. On social occasions, when other family members or guests were about, Nancy did not make any effort to insert herself and she was able to eventually become accustom to the unspoken reality of such gatherings. People were kind and she was always deferential.

As Washington grew, he too became familiar with the practices expected for his life. Nancy guarded against any effort on his part to be aware of a superior attitude or an effort to assume the superiority of preferential treatment not afforded to other slave children. It was the demon that lurked in the shadow and Nancy was ever vigilant.

Two years later, Sidney was born, then Robert Pinckney, then Henry Clay. Nancy had her own cabin and it was becoming filled with children. Not by announcement but by the creation of a family, Josiah made evident to his

84

extended family, his intention to maintain his relationship with Nancy.

Elizabeth and Frances lived in the main house and Josiah took a direct involvement with their upbringing. Their grandfather died but Rhoda was their female influence. She saw to it that in practice, the community knew the girls were Josiah's children without ever allowing his mulatto children to come into the general conversation.

Judge Thomas Settle had built his home about a mile west of the David Settle home place along the road that stayed south of the Dan River and ran toward the lower fords of the Dan near Danville. It was in the front yard of that home that he had a large one room brick schoolhouse built for his children and neighbors and relations. His daughters, Mary Martin's two daughters and Josiah's two daughters were allowed to attend but not Josiah's children by Nancy. Josiah made arrangements to give his mulatto children a modest education which was against the state law at the time. Clandestine as that was, Josiah ignored the law with the complicity of the other Settle families. This practice of condoning exceptions to laws that had been created to perpetuate the onerous system, contributed to the friction of the social extremes. The more that families in leadership functioned by going around the law, the more the law was left to sustain slavery. The law itself became the source of the social hypocrisy and religion found a way to provide the justification.

When Thomas would come to visit his widowed mother, he and Josiah would usually have a prickly conversation. If Thomas had brought some of his children, they might be found playing with Josiah's white daughters or his children by Nancy.

"Well Josiah, I see you now have two more, William Harrison and Winfield Scott. If you and Nancy keep going, you will be able to honor every leader of the Whig Party."

Although Thomas was smiling, Josiah understood the insult casually delivered. "Well you see Tom, since my actions are not contingent on political or social propriety, I am able to provide my children respectable names. That way there is no embarrassment to you in using family names."

"Thank you," replied Thomas.

"You have no doubt heard that I have purchased a large plantation in Mississippi in the old Chickasaw Territory. It lies in the northeast corner adjoining Alabama, Tishomingo County. It's on the Tombigbee River"

"Mary says that Robert Martin has purchased land in Lawrence County, Mississippi, down on the Pearl River. That must be far south of you. I dare say that before long half of North Carolina will be off to Mississippi or to Texas."

"There are fortunes to be had and none too soon as the soil around here seems running out."

Tom's loyalty to his home state was challenged but he did not want to sound defensive. After all, if Josiah were to move his brood to Mississippi there might be some awkward pressure removed from the family around here. 'That sounded unkind, even to him,' he thought. Then to be plain spoken he asked, "Do you intend on removing to Mississippi?"

"At the moment, I intend on investment. One thing certainty does strongly influence me though. I do not want to purchase a lot more slaves and in order to gain from the ownership of rich cotton land, I will need even more slave labor than I employ in North Carolina."

"That seems to be a common consideration for many who believe that riches are to be made in the Cotton South. Cotton is more labor intensive than growing tobacco. In my opinion, the opening of the Indian lands and thus the productivity of the Cotton South, has doomed any reasonable negotiated end to slavery. I find it a great sadness."

"It is a dilemma that I have. My heart yearns for the end of slavery but am I exacerbating the problem and making inevitable the crisis?"

"I am pleased that you can at least see the conundrum, Josiah. I suppose none of us individually can bring about an end of slavery. Oh, perhaps Senator Douglas can, but not men like me. You know, there is a classic example of the dilemma. Douglas married Martha Martin, the single heiress of a plantation owner with several hundred slaves in North Carolina and Mississippi, the single commodity that his politics dictates he cannot have. He married wealth but at what price? I believe it is more temptation than even Adam faced.

"You also have a quandary, Josiah. Do you not? A white plantation owner with two white daughters, a black family by a slave woman, and a large company of slaves, to which you add a labor hungry cotton plantation; that all seems to cover more social variables than a single man should be able to balance."

"Thank you for your kind reminder but you forgot an aging widowed mother.'

"Don't take on more than is necessary. Mary and I can take good care of mother."

"Thomas, I wish that talking with you could bring me more obvious alternatives. Instead you only remind me, more succinctly every time, that I am surrounded by predicaments. Then I am reminded that my Nancy is not only the half sister of my late Frances but also of your dear Henrietta. I fear that poor Nancy is my responsibility but your burden. Who has the dilemma?"

Josiah began to appreciate his plantation in Mississippi as the potential path for his deliverance. North Carolina and Virginia were known for the quality of their tobacco product in spite of the fact that constant re-use was depleting the soil. There were more tobacco factories in Rockingham County than in any other county in the state. Their production had been packed on wagons and peddled by younger sons throughout the lower South for several generations. That is how Josiah had gotten his first introduction to Mississippi.

The Christmas Day Rabbit Hunt for the Settle men was a tradition. There had not been snow for several weeks but it had been cold so even though snow remained around the edges of the fields, the open ground was clear and frozen hard. The sky was cloudless and there was little wind. It was a perfect day to go hunting.

In 1846 Washington, Josiah's eldest son by Nancy, was sixteen. As a special recognition of his age, he was to be allowed to accompany his father, not to shot but to carry the shotgun and help gather up the rabbits. It was also the first time that one of the traditions within the Settle family was going to be shared with any member of Josiah's mulatto family. In a very subtle way it was a coming out. There was no objection because it could be pretended that the men were just taking along a slave to help with the hunt. No questions asked.

Josiah had instructed Washington that he should stay right with him and not to wander. His mother had been terribly afraid that he was too young for such a hunting party but she had been given little voice. Washington would have agreed to any conditions just to be allowed to go along.

In the first three hours of hunting they had been able to kill nine rabbits which seemed only modestly successful because rabbits had been out everywhere. The banter had turned to challenges and disparaging comments about missed shots.

Josiah was letting Washington carry his empty shotgun after he had discharged it and when they prepared for another firing he sometimes let Washington load the gun. If Josiah hit a rabbit Washington would run out in the field with the dogs to round up the carcasses.

About one o'clock Josiah fired and saw that he had hit a rabbit. Without thinking, he handed the gun to

Washington so the boy could reload. Other members of the group were still firing and Washington went to his task with deliberation. When the others had finished their shooting, and without looking around, Josiah called to Washington to go and help round up the dead rabbits. The boy instinctively ran forward without being aware that he still had the gun which was now loaded. When he was half way across the field, Josiah noted that he had the gun and called out, "Washington, bring that gun back here."

Washington realized what he was doing and turned abruptly to run back and tripped on an unstable clod of dirt. His body twisted. He spun in the air and he clutched the gun. As gun and boy came down together, the gun fired. Josiah knew what had happened. He and several of the others rushed forward but Josiah arrived at his son first. He saw immediately that the full blast had gone through the boy's body. He cried out, "Oh! God!"

Nancy had heard the shooting begin soon after they had left the house. She was uneasy from that moment. She watched for their return. As she passed by each window in the main house, she would glance toward the fields. She was the first to see Josiah walking slowly toward the house carrying Washington and followed by a clutch of men.

She ran through the house and from the front door screaming denial. "Not my boy! Not my boy," she called. "Oh God. Not my boy." Josiah collapsed in the yard, squatting with the child in his lap,

Nancy reached them and on her knees began a kind of struggle with Josiah for the bloody body of their son. The others were gentle as they tried to calm the terror of

90

emotion. There was no way. The energy was grief beyond containment.

The Settles, and most of their relations through marriage, came together through the depth of this tragedy. Color seemed such a trifling consideration. An innocent child had died and the grief had no boundaries. Thomas and Henrietta particularly sought to grieve with Josiah and Nancy. Their oldest son, Thomas, was only a year younger than Washington. They had played as children. They were blood relations.

He was buried with the family, not with old David or with Frances Settle but a little further out along the ridge. Josiah insisted that he should 'have a fine headstone,' that would tell the world why there was so much grief in the loss of this child. Such material acts of grief are rarely palliative - important at the time but rarely do they contribute to the process.

There was an unspoken issue mixed into this process of grief for Josiah and Nancy. It made for a special loneliness. Their human suffering had to play out in the context of a social order that was based on separation by race. Their eldest child, their son, was the product of the mixing of those races, committed by them.

Chapter 3

Grief is catalytic. For Josiah and Nancy it exposed as raw all those contradictions that besieged their life together, those they had passively ignored. The world beyond their families, they had simply been able to disregard. Within their families, they had developed scenarios of understanding: tense banter with Thomas and distance with Henrietta, disapproval with Robert Martin but benign blessing from Mary, and resentment from Azariah and the Graves family for perpetuating a sin that long since should have been covered up. Washington's death had thrust them forward onto the stage. They were no longer part of a supporting cast but their very presence on the family stage forced other cast members to play their parts around them and in their presence.

Josiah could function as master. He could demand his place at the plantation table. Nancy was a slave. She had no resource to which she could turn with confidence. Caring for her other children, nurturing, was a balm but it did not heal the wound. It always came back to the wound. Each action, every event, came back to the wound.

Nancy miscarried. For days she was mildly catatonic. She could feed herself, feed her children but there was no cognitive appreciation of the act. She sat and spoke but did not communicate.

She found reason to begin to recover with the prospect of a marriage between her oldest step-daughter, Elizabeth Graves, and Dr. Henry Allen Howard of Caswell

County. The prospect of joy quickly became another cause for disappointment. Once again, she was a former Graves slave, not Josiah Settle's wife or the mother of his children, all half-brothers and sisters of the bride. She was not welcome except to serve after the ceremony.

Josiah made another of his biennial trips to the plantation in Tishomingo. En-route he had considered, then decided, that it was no longer possible for Nancy to find any peace in North Carolina. He made plans to expand the overseer's house on the Mississippi plantation to better suit the size of his family. He also served himself by making it more fitting for a plantation master. He had a hundred slaves there already and he would divest himself of all his land and interests in North Carolina and bring his fifty slaves from there. He didn't think he would have to add any slaves.

His chief concern was, if this would be enough to overcome the restrictive forces that burdened Nancy. In Mississippi he could not provide her or their children their freedom any more than he could in North Carolina. Manumission was legal in either state but meant that persons freed had one year to leave the state. Still then, his promise when they were married, to free Nancy and all her children, was blocked by the law. Could Mississippi ever be anything more than a half-way point along a road that had to lead to manumission?

On his return, Josiah found the moment when he could advise Nancy of the plans he had made. To his surprise, her response was immediately positive.

"Josiah, I have wondered myself if we could ever be happier in Mississippi. I heard your enthusiasm about the productivity of the soil but I was immediately concerned that slavery might be even harsher there than here. Would my children be any better off. I knew that I wanted to go. I had to get away from here. It is too painful when people you should love, disappoint you in so many cruel ways. If for no other reason, I am sure I must get away from that."

"You cannot run from your fears, Nancy. They will follow you."

"Yes, but they won't be in constant confrontation. Distance can be some relief."

"We will be leaving Washington here, you know."

"And you will be leaving Frances but it will have to be. What of your daughters? You will be leaving them."

"They have helped me make up my mind to pursue this move. Elizabeth has married Dr. Howard. I do not think that they will stay in Caswell but they will choose where his practice might be most promising. Frances is being heavily courted by her cousin, John Hinton Graves and I dare say they will soon marry. They are leaving me. "

"They should always be happy with us, Josiah."

It was several months before Josiah announced their intentions within the family and he made clear that the move would be in stages. His interest in the family estate needed to be clarified and he intended to dispose of land in North Carolina.

There was little shock in the reaction he received. Actually he realized that what he saw in their response, was

94

their effort to cover up their relief and then their guilt for even having those feelings.

The plan was to go in the fall, toward the end of the crop year in North Carolina and before fall planting in Mississippi. Then Azariah Graves, the old General, died. The most emotionally bitter relationships were exercised. Nancy was not welcome to attend the funeral of her father. She was a contradiction to the family dynamics. Josiah was the widowed son-in-law, so he had to attend. Henrietta Settle was the old man's daughter so she and Thomas would certainly attend. But Nancy was only Azariah's daughter by a slave. Too many people knew. Her presence would be abrasive and unwelcome. She stayed with her children in the slave quarters of the old Settle place - in her place. Was this same feeling of being such an outsider going to be raised by every marriage and funeral in the Settle family? It was a depressing prospect.

Soon after the funeral, Nancy realized that she was again pregnant. When she told Josiah, she was prepared.

"I am strong, Josiah, and we can make the trip in the fall as planned."

"Impossible! We shall make the trip in the next spring."

Nancy protested but recognized that she would have to have her way by degrees, over time. She pushed Josiah to continue to make the necessary moves to clear his business dealings. She prepared the children for the prospect of the move. When the will of Azariah Graves made no mention of her, she was furious but she accepted the disappointment as another confirmation that they must

95

go. At some point Josiah began speaking in terms of a September departure and Nancy knew she had prevailed.

Rockingham County had seen many summers when families disposed of their interests in North Carolina and assembled wagons and buggies, all sorts of rolling stock, good productive livestock, and a coffle of their slaves, and departed south. Josiah had placed most of his family in the older of the Settle carriages and put the older of his children in a following wagon with two slave women in supervision. Their wagon could be easily covered. Furniture and equipment wagons followed, sparingly packed but sufficient to all their needs when they reached Mississippi. The livestock were herded behind the slaves.

The day was warm and the leaves were showing spots of color in upper branches. There had not been anything like a frost. Sadness, anticipation, joy, fear, foreboding, and grief mixed in the air. The family itself constituted a crowd but there were many neighbors as well, present to see the departure. Most realized that they would likely never see each other again. Saying goodbye was physical, hugging and kissing, tears and some forced laughs.

The train started, one after the other beginning to move. They were watched over the hill to the west as they disappeared, a wagon at a time. They moved west until they joined the lower road when it crossed Big Troublesome. They passed through Salem and instead of turning south toward Salisbury, they turned towards the mountains and to Tennessee.

Nancy was doing well even seven months into her pregnancy. The children were all warming to the adventure. The mountains were difficult particularly on the animals and the slaves. Josiah had no reason to rush as long as the weather held. They reached Knoxville by mid-month and pushed forward to Nashville where they would pick up the Natchez Trace.

South of Nashville, Nancy went into labor. It appeared that she might have been further along in her pregnancy than they had thought. She had given birth many times and they had barely time to reach a tavern on the road, after her water broke. The baby was a boy, a little smaller than her other sons had been but well formed and apparently very healthy. Nancy was overjoyed. The child was a signal to her that life was returning and they would find greater happiness when they reached their destination.

"You have given each child a name, Josiah. Some I admit I did not fully understand but I came to realize that you were avoiding the use of any of the names used by your family. This child I want to name. I want to call him Josiah Thomas Settle. He will proudly carry your name and your brother's and he will be a Settle.

After two days of rest, Nancy and the baby seemed robust and the journey was resumed. They crossed the Tennessee River at Colbert's Ferry then left the Trace and swung back northwest to their destination in Tishomingo on the Tombigbee River, Mississippi.

Josiah Settle (1799-1869) Greenwood Cemetery, Hamilton, OH Nancy Ann Graves (1815-1893), tombstone Eldorado, Preble County, OH

On October 7, 1850, Josiah completed the final purchase from Samuel and Fatinia Flake, of Section #12, Township and Range # 6.

Chapter 4

The conscious feeling of release came to Josiah and Nancy in small ways. In Tishomingo, they and their children were the Settle family. There was no need to identify their relationship to someone else named Settle. They were more isolated, surrounded by large plantations many with non-resident owners. Their plantation, including mulattos and slaves, could exist on their own terms. They needed no approval, asked or offered.

Basically they felt self-sufficient at first. Then the question of the education of the children surfaced. There was no schooling for slaves. Josiah could find no tutor who would live in their home and teach the children. Nancy found that having herself driven to the post office and store at Boneyard by a slave, did not make her mistress of the plantation, as were the others women who shopped.

Still, the newness of the place kept everyone busy. Josiah had crops to set and more quarters to be built. New fields were opened by the slaves he had brought from North Carolina. Nancy had the opportunity to create the management of the household and the care of the children. She immediately found that her implied status of mistress did not sit well with other slaves who considered her no more than one of them. Oversight of the children meant that she tried to provide more for her children than was there for other slave children. That created an awkward separation.

Cotton was driving a world marketplace and most years in the decade produced bumper crops accelerating that market. As Nancy had feared, slavery was even more a concern and issue in Mississippi. In spite of the labor saving of the invention of the cotton gin, the population of slaves now exceeded that of whites. That produced an attitude of uneasiness.

Josiah was immersed in creating a robust cotton plantation. He intended to take advantage of the economic boom. His choice to invest in Mississippi land had proven to be wise and his prospects promised to underwrite the future of his family.

For Nancy, the abundant prospects for Josiah had replaced the burden she had experienced in North Carolina among the stifling surroundings of the extended Settle family. She had not been liberated. Slave she was and slave she feared she would always be.

Friction crept into every small corner of their lives. Nancy knew that Josiah had been a successful slave trader before he first married. When she was depressed, feeling that she and her children never would be free, she would ask herself, has he always intended to keep us in slavery? Is he just a slaver at heart? The prospects that their children were always going to be limited as long as they were slaves, gnawed at her. Nancy could pretend that this was her house but to all the slaves that surrounded her, she was a slave just like they were. She was Nancy, not Mrs. Settle. What did she expect?

This time, there was no catalyst. One day Nancy simply said, "When will we be free?"

Josiah knew in an instant that he was the one who had to act. He could tell Nancy that she would always be a slave but then he was consigning his children to the same fate. He would have been breaking his long ago pledge to her but he could not see his children forever in slavery.

Nancy had made it business. She had called his hand. They had to be free even if it meant that they could not live in Mississippi. Agreeing to manumission meant they had to leave. As was his previous practice, he deliberated alone for some time. Then he brought his findings, full blown, to Nancy.

"My investment is here in Mississippi. My slaves make up over half of the value of my estate. If I sacrifice either land or slaves, I will lose the financial stability that I intended to use for the future of our family."

Nancy thought that was unfair. Suddenly she and her children threatened Josiah's planned stability.

"We must examine our future as a family separately. You will be free. I have made you that promise and our children are owed freedom as part of the heritage that I can give them. It exercises my soul. How can I be the source of my children's freedom and leave more than a hundred black persons in slavery? I know Nancy, that is my cross to carry and I will not burden you or the children with it."

"What you are saying also says that we must go but wherever we shall go, we must go as a family," defined Nancy.

"I have been planning a trip north to buy some equipment. I had thought to see Indiana, Ohio, and perhaps Illinois. I will be able to investigate sites that I think might suit us. I can travel north on steamboats on the Tennessee

101

and up the Ohio. If I find what we desire near the Ohio, I will easily travel between that location and the plantation here in Mississippi. I will be an absentee owner but I think I can be more directly a part of management than most."

Among a number of locations, Josiah's 1856 trip took him to Butler County, Ohio, just above Cincinnati. He made a connection there to supply his equipment needs and was so cordially treated that he purchased an available house.

On his return to Mississippi, Josiah was able to paint for Nancy the picture of a promised fulfillment. He was certain that they would be welcomed in Hanover Township and as husband and wife. All the series of barriers, legal and societal, that had plagued their relationship, would be behind them.

First he made the necessary arrangement for Nancy and all her children to be freed, including the youngest, Josephine, born to her in Mississippi. They would depart the state in the spring after planting was complete and they would pass as free people out of the slave states and by water, enter their new home in Ohio. They took the train from the port on the Ohio River at Cincinnati directly to Hanover Station on the Cincinnati, Hamilton & Dayton Railroad. Their furniture followed shortly after. The Township station was so close they could walk the single block to their new home.

From the time he had announced their move to Ohio, Josiah had referred to this house as Nancy's house. They both understood him to mean that since he would be much of the time in Mississippi managing the plantation, Nancy would be able to manage her own home.

Upon their arrival, they were warmly welcomed. Then it became known that they had never been married. Behind closed doors, the locals were horrified. The fact that Josiah and Nancy were a mixed race couple did not disturb them but they could not be accepted unless they were married. Nancy resisted, feeling that they had always been married in the sight of God. Josiah bought a second house for himself, for the sake of propriety. His neighbors were still unsatisfied.

Josiah became exasperated and finally claimed, "Marriage, that is what I have always wanted."

He and Nancy argued. Both knew this was unacceptable but neither wanted to again have to succumb to rules and standards set by other people.

"I have finally overcome slavery only to be throttled with my neighbor's rules of what constitutes an acceptable marriage. Can we have no peace?"

Marriage Josiah Settle & Nancy Settle

Most people were more sensitive and wanted to help plan the wedding and it seemed like an acceptable act considering what they had already been through. On May 31, 1858 Josiah and Nancy Graves Settle were married by Rev. H. M. Richardson. Their children were witness to the service by which, in the eyes of society, they became legitimate.

For almost thirty years Josiah Settle had maintained an intimate relationship with Nancy, a slave of his late wife. They had produced ten children between them. This was to be the third structure of their long relationship. Nancy would live in the house Josiah had bought for her with the younger children. He would live in the house next door with the older children until they married. Part of the year he lived in Mississippi and cared for his plantation and the rest he spent in Ohio.

War was clearly on the way. Josiah, a Unionist from his days in North Carolina, could not defend slavery. Although he had hoped that the plantation would give security to his family, he knew that if war came he would possibly lose the plantations anyway. He sold his Mississippi land and slaves in 1860 and returned to Ohio. Josiah and Nancy never lived together again. Their relations were much as they had always been and the children seemed accustomed in flowing seamlessly between the house of their mother and that of their father. The children were now able to be well educated in the local schools.

Josiah Settle died in Hanover Township in 1869.

BOOK V
THOMAS SETTLE, UNIONIST

Chapter 1

It was April 14, 1861. Judge George Howard and Thomas Settle, Solicitor of the Fourth Judicial District, took no note that they had just passed into Rockingham County. Yesterday Howard had allowed Superior Court in Stokes County to be adjourned and debate to be held between Unionist and Secessionist candidates. Settle and J. M. Leach, a Randolph County attorney, had spoken for the Unionists. Alfred Moore Scales, Jr., and Robert McLean of Guilford represented the Secessionists. The courthouse audience of Stokes seemed almost evenly divided. Debate had been friendly, between fellow attorneys who were identified, not by the old party labels but as to their position on the single matter that consumed them all - secession.

Tom Settle was a Democrat due largely to the influence of his brother-in-law, David Settle Reid, who had lost his seat in the US Senate two years earlier. He had been the first Governor elected as a Democratic in the state (1851-1854). Almost a generation older than Tom, David Reid established the Democratic Party control in North Carolina. Settle had been Governor Reid's private secretary until he had entered the bar in 1854.

It had been Reid who as Governor had supported former Governor John M. Morehead in the establishment of the North Carolina Central Railroad. The quarrels over railroad charters and the pressure from Secessionists and Abolitionists had constituted most of the political debate in North Carolina in the decade before the Civil War. Although both issues, the railroad and secession, were debated in the state, it was the marriage of Settle and Reid's first cousin, Martha Martin to Senator Stephen A. Douglas of Illinois, that brought a dominating national dialogue to the extended family of Martin, Settle, and Reid on the Dan River in North Carolina.

Settle and Judge Howard rode quietly across a sloping meadow where fields had been prepared to receive young tobacco plants. As a conversation starter, Judge Howard ventured, "I suspect that we settled nothing in the debate yesterday, Tom. You and Leach were convincing but Scales and McLean have anger and prejudice in their favor. I see throughout the state the appeal to such emotions, clothed in patriotism and pride and honor, to be coalescing. Politicians are surrendering to demagoguery as easy sources of popularity. I am amazed that for so long this country has been able to avoid the inevitable rupture that we enshrined in our Constitutional document. For eighty-five years we have been hung on slavery's cross and been whistling through the dark in the hope that a miracle would save us."

"A colorful analysis, Judge Howard," said Settle. "I know not of miracles but I believe that as long as we can protect the Union, we can negotiate a compromise. I am less certain that we can find an end to slavery without a war of decision.

"You may know that Scales is my personal and political nemesis. We are about two years apart in age and were born only a few miles apart. We went to the same school, a little brick school in front of my parent's house near Reidsville. We went to the University and he left to

107

have an unfortunate marriage to a woman in Louisiana. I got my degree in 1850 about the time he had returned to Rockingham County to set up a law office in Madison. In '56 we were both in the legislature. I guess it was inevitable that competition in our youth was to hang over into our competition as attorneys and then as politicians. It seemed a natural rub but there has never been any malice."

"I have seen it before when two men have run so close from birth and have chosen a common profession. They seem to have inbred competition. I hope you and Scales will always refrain from bitterness."

The buggy rose along the grade, Tom's horse hitched to the rear. As they crested this last hill, Tom scanned in the horizon the valley of Dan River. "Look there," he cried suddenly and swung his upper body out of the side of the buggy so as to stand. "There in the distance. a secession flag flying over Madison. Something has happened. Madison is a Union town. There must be news."

As he spoke, two riders approached up the hill. "What news," Tom shouted? "There is a 'secesh' flag."

"Sumpter has been fired upon. Lincoln has called for 75,000 troops from North Carolina. Everybody is for war!"

"Governor Reid is speaking in Madison," said the second rider. "Volunteers are enlisting."

Tom swung back in place. "I must get to Madison," he shouted with painful animation.

"Calm yourself, sir. You will have time enough for that."

"I must go now, Judge. I cannot be seen to linger."
He leapt from the slowing buggy, unleashed his horse and
threw on the saddle. By the time Howard stopped, Tom was
in full gallop. Howard proceeded at a lesser pace.

Gov. David Settle Reid outside Capitol, Raleigh
NC Department of Archives and History

The porch of 'Trader Black's' Hotel jutted out to the
edge of Murphey Street in Madison. From the second story,
Reid was holding forth.

"We have withheld the hand of war. We have tried
the path of compromise in all its forms. We have been
rejected in all our attempts to remain part of our Union. We
seek no enemies in our brothers and sisters in the North but
neither will we fire against our neighbor states." Scanning
beyond the crowd, Reid pointed. "Yonder comes Thomas
Settle. Let him through. We will hear from him."

David Settle Reid (1813-1891)

Library of Congress

Thomas knew that Scales had his law office in Madison and he hoped that, since he had seen him still in the streets in Danbury when he and Judge Howard were leaving, he had not had time to get to Madison. He was desperate to speak first.

"Friends! I was all wrong," he began in half breath. Again, "I was ALL wrong! You were right. I counted Union too dear and so did many of you. Now we can see that there was no compromise to be had. Northern Radicals intended to destroy the South by destroying our economy in any way. They did not seek freedom for the Negro. Lincoln, like Pilate himself, would wipe away the stains of his own sin. Cry as he might, 'I do not want war,' his every action was bringing on war as if pre-planned.

"Now, North Carolina must join with her southern sister states in a second confederation. The first has been taken from us. We must make an even more perfect Union. Just as in 1776, we must defend it against those who would seek to subjugate us. There is no liberty for anyone if we

110

are denied freedom of action. It is our right - NO, it is our RESPONSIBILITY to defend our right to independent action."

Thomas Settle was at his impressive best. His voice had been cultivated in the debating societies at the University. His modulated voice was known to seize the emotions of an audience and escort them to his purpose. His eyes were dark and intense and seemed ignited by a cause. This speech was extemporaneous but ordinarily he would meticulously work out his remarks on paper so as to more perfectly weave ideas into some kind of symmetry.

"Brothers and sisters, we are called to sacrifice so that we can be victorious over this aggression that has been made upon us. We will all suffer. Our brave young men will do their duty. They will rally to a new flag of freedom. They will defend the flowers of our Southland, our women and our children, against the Yankee aggression.

"Men, prepare your vineyards! Go home and plant your crops and mend your fences. Then rally to our flag to defend your freedom. Leave your families to the harvest as you turn toward the enemy with the certainty that men of all ages have had when they faced another aggression. You are defending your birthright. God will sustain you. Your families will pray for you. You will know VICTORY!"

Cheers had punctuated his words again and again and as he flung up his arms, a sustained roar filled the valley. He saw nothing of Scales so he indeed had been able to grasp the mantle of patriotism before his rival. It was no small personal victory. Had Scales been first to speak, he would certainly have pressed Union like a crown of thorns upon Settle's head. With one speech, Settle had assumed the mantle of the Confederacy. Scales was left with saying, "me too."

Chapter 2

Settle and Judge Howard left the madness at Madison to go to Settle's home down river on the Dan. His father, Judge Settle, had bought the home of another Alfred Moore Scales, uncle of Tom's competitor, and given it to Tom. It was another interfamily wound since the elder A. M. Scales had sold his Mulberry Island plantation as the result of a bankruptcy. The Scales family had suffered a number of financial reverses in the decade of the 1850s forcing more than one caravan of loaded wagons and slave coffles to begin their way south to the cotton fields of Alabama and Mississippi. Many of the more prominent Virginia and North Carolina plantation owners had been forced into bankruptcy as their tobacco fields, worn out by years of repeated cultivation, had become less productive. Periodic financial depressions would tip the scales on farms that were only marginally fertile.

Still, there was residual bitterness in bankruptcy when land and slaves had been the measure of a farmer's financial worth. Only the most substantial farms had been given particular names and when bankruptcy made public the loss and sale of such a plantation, it was an embarrassment for all of that family. Mulberry Island, 'the Scale's Place', was bought by Judge Settle and given to Thomas. The humiliation was unspoken. It was only masked in part by the flow of so many other families out of North Carolina to the Cotton South.

Judge Howard had to literally extricate Settle from the adoring crowd in Madison. It was becoming a riotous mob

113

and many were already armed for something, they knew not what. The effect had noticeably disconcerted young Settle. His fixed stare had an unconscious appearance. Howard attempted to revive his wits. "The die is surely cast. There is no way that it can be recovered. We are committed to the Confederacy."

Settle remained inert, in his own world. He had heard Howard and processed his word without any outward evidence. "I will resign my office and go into the army," he finally declared calmly.

"You are overwrought, Thomas. You are a man of deliberation and what you are saying now is all emotion. You have a home and new wife and daughter - personal responsibilities. You hold a critical public office. This is not the time to surrender to emotion."

"You are wrong, Judge Howard. This is a defining moment. What each of us chooses is going to define our future. It is as if at this moment, we begin again. It is a time of declaration. I have seen my commitment to Union trampled in the dust."

"You can still be a force of reason, Thomas. The times require some voice of reason."

"There will be a time that will seek reason, Judge, but it will only come now after we have mixed the blood of North and South on some unnamed battlefield."

They had been seen approaching along the River Road and Mary stood in the yard holding Henrietta. Judge Settle came out of the house as they dismounted from the buggy.

Thomas Settle, Jr. (1831-1888)

"Take my horse," said Thomas to his slave, Dick as he unhitched the bridle and tossed it over. "Then unhitch the buggy and feed both horses."

He turned toward his wife. Mary was noticeably frightened and apprehensive. The Judge waited.

"It is war," declared Thomas. "Lincoln has called for troops. I have declared in Madison." He moved to take Mary and the baby in his arms. "Judge will you please give them the details?"

Later, on the veranda, having fielded all the denials and pleading, Thomas was able to lay out what he considered to be his only honorable course. At first he was harsh with himself, bemoaning his tenacious commitment to preservation of the Union.

"As a family, we have been defined by a cause that was right, Thomas," his father stated firmly. "Do not question that. You and David Reid and I have championed a view of Union. Don't forget Senator Douglas. The debate within our family has been the reasoned position - until this moment. I am convinced. Even in the face of these altered circumstances we are not required to repudiate what we have held as legitimate. It is not we who have given up on the Union. Southern radicals in our midst and Abolitionists who have subsumed our President, have succeeded in shattering the national trust.

"We must react as with new circumstances. We can no longer defend a chain of Union that has been shattered. We are a Southern state, economically, socially, historically. Our loyalty must be to the South."

116

"The tragedy, father, is that we are also the region of slavery. Lincoln has succeeded in nailing us to the cross of slavery. We start a nation branded with sin. My agony is to believe that we do not defend slavery but the sacred right of statehood, to self-determination. Is that folly?"

One week later, Monday the 20th, court week for Rockingham County was scheduled. The milling swarm of people present at Wentworth made it clear that there could be no court. No building in town could hope to contain such a crowd. Families had come to deliver their sons to 'the cause.' Young men, some wearing pieces of uniforms from past wars or with weapons carried by their ancestors, waited for a voice of authority. A jumble of musicians played rasping military music.

Wheeler Hancock, a noble veteran of the Mexican War, stepped forward and hushed the gathering. Looking about, he spotted Thomas Settle and Alfred Moore Scales and summoned them forward. Placing them on either side, he called in a loud voice, "Gentlemen, form into ranks behind Scales or Settle."

It took several minutes of unorganized shuffling before two distinct groups stood awkwardly at attention. "Today you will become Company H and Company I of the 13th North Carolina Regiment of the Army of the Confederate States. Until you are formally organized, Company H will be led by Scales and Company I will be led by Settle."

So war began.

Chapter 3

The Rockingham Guards under Alfred Scales and the Rockingham Rangers under Thomas Settle were organized at Garysburg in Northampton County and then crossed the border to Suffolk and were mustered into Confederate service on June 1, 1861. By August, they were moved into positions along the James River and during their period in Winter Quarters the regiment was re-designated the 13th Regiment of N. C. Troops. Having enlisted, both Scales and Settle had been given Company commands as Captains

At the time of the re-designation in October, Scales was elected Colonel and was transferred to the Field and Staff of the regiment. Then on April 26, 1862, Settle was re-elected Captain but refused and 'went home,' to be replaced by Chalmers Glenn.

Glenn had been adopted by his widowed uncle, Dr. E. T. Brodnax at Lower Sauratown and was raising his children there. Settle's younger brother, David, was a Lieutenant in Company H, and when he was denied reelection on the same day his brother resigned, he quit the army also.

"My actions will not bring me glory, Captain Glenn," Tom Settle admitted to Chalmers Glenn, "but I also hope they will not constitute dishonor." They were talking in Settle's tent soon after Settle had told his second in command of his intended resignation. "The election today has demonstrated that politics, of a most partial kind, rules every army."

"Of course it does, Tom. We are a collection of citizen soldiers and it is natural that we bring to our army much of our local politics. Our boys have not seen battle, so when they are given the opportunity to choose their officers, they cannot judge on the basis of courage or leadership. They can expectedly resort to old politics. But Tom, you were re-elected in the face of the pettiness of the election."

"In October I saw Scales promoted to Colonel and advanced to regimental staff. On what basis, I ask you? Now, another election and Henry McGehee is defeated as Scales' replacement and Dave is passed over as Lieutenant. I am pleased that you will be my replacement in this company but I will not serve under Scales.

"I have disagreed with Alf Scales since we were boys. In recent years he has been an open defender of slavery in our state. Oh, he defended it in the guise of secession but it is obvious that this war is in fact a shameful defense of slavery. He is among those who would hang that curse around the neck of an honorable Christian people. See how he is rewarded and because I fought to preserve the Union, I am preserved as a Captain.

"I will not lead young men into battle and even to death, for his cause. I was willing to defer my principles and lead my fellow citizens in patriotic fervor but on that basis, I will not follow that man. My friends know that I am as much a patriot as is Scales."

"I can understand your emotions, Tom, but if you leave the field to Scales, he will be able to claim the victory of this war and you will be forgotten."

119

"He can have his victory, if victory there be and he can manage with defeat if that is the end. I don't see glory. I will no longer ask men to die in defense of slavery. That is not the way this war started but it is the poison that men like Scales now use to confuse men who are asked to die, most of whom have no slaves. Rally the men, Chalmers, I must make them understand."

"Sir, no man has the respect of his men as do you. If this army is to be victorious, we must have men like you in command."

"That is the sentiment of a friend whom I hold dear, Captain Glenn. It is men like you that we must have when this war is over in order to bind up the state and rebuild a new type of economy. I pray earnestly that you will be spared, my friend."

Company I was assembled, at ease. Settle stepped forward. The utter silence made clear that rumors already had carried the news he was about to give.

"Men, I have made the most difficult decision of my life. I am about to take the most fateful action that a soldier can take but I cannot proceed without advising the men that I have led as a soldier and as friend for this past year. I find myself unable to continue to command under the assignment fallen to me in this army. For that reason, within the hour, I will resign my commission and become a private citizen of North Carolina." There is a soft murmur since this is not news but a confirmation of a rumor.

"My love for this army and for you brave men is boundless but I find myself unable to reject my own principle of faith and human dignity. I cannot defend the

120

one at the expense of the other. I will return to Rockingham County and I will serve whenever and wherever the people see me useful. When this war is over, I swear to you, that I will move heaven and earth to restore our state to peace and harmony. For the rest of my days, I will hold each one of you as precious in my heart. I will gladly defend you with my life but I can no longer command you as part of this army. 'Forgive me my trespasses.'"

Settle was surrounded by men he had trained but he had not led them in battle. In a back corner of the sympathetic crowd one soldier turned to another. "Easy enough for him to go home and we face the shot and shell."

Chapter 4

At the Sauratown, the air of mourning hung deep. It had taken four days for news to reach the family that Captain Chalmers Glenn had been killed at a Battle near South Mountain in Maryland. Ann Dodge Glenn was shattered but stoic. She was able to keep her pain at a distance as she attempted to accommodate the insecurity of three little boys. James Dodge was 10, Robert Brodnax was 8, and Edward Travis had just celebrated his third birthday a week before. The child had been so proud of the Union cap his father had sent him from the battlefield.

"Each of us has his own bitter sadness today," Settle said to Dr. Edward Travis Brodnax. They stood in the parlor of the imposing home the doctor had erected on the site of the old Belview house at the Sauratown. Faced with yellow brick brought from England, this house was an imposing statement of the Brodnax' wealth but today it was filled with the sorrow of fateful tragedy that was rapidly enshrouding the South.

"I find some solace in my bitterness, Tom." E.T. was not a buoyant spirit. He was a widower when he adopted Chalmers Glenn, succumbing to the pleading of Chalmer's mother, his dying sister-in-law. Brodnax and his wife were childless. He was good at managing his plantation and his medical practice was of such repute that young men hoping to become Doctors, came from good families all over North Carolina and southern Virginia to work under him.

"Chalmers always made me proud," he mused. "I had wondered if a widower could take on such a responsibility but Tom Gallaway could not take him at Rose Hill." Lucinda Gallaway was Sarah Glenn's other sister.

"He would have made his mark, I am certain of that. He was far better with relationships. People were naturally attracted to his personality. The message said he was 'a very gallant officer.' Should we bring him back home?"

E.T.'s question was almost absent minded, addressed to no one in particular.

"Time enough for that," replied Settle so that the question would not hang.

Enoch had brought some brandy. Mourners were arriving now from a distance. Tyre and Margaret Glenn, parents of Settle's wife, came from Yadkin County. Tyre was a slave trader but shared opposition to secession with Settle. Settle acknowledged them briefly then returned to his conversation with Dr. Brodnax.

"You know that I am struggling today with the unease that I somehow deserted him, left him to command," continued Settle. "Had I stayed in April, might he be alive and might this wake be in my honor? It is morbid, I understand but the wonder sits there unresolved. Perhaps it will never be resolved - a cross indeed."

E.T. looked up and was taught in directing a response. "You were both soldiers and made choices. Chalmers spoke when last we saw him, about the agony that surrounded your departure from the army - yours and your men. He was, however, deeply admiring of your convictions. He told me he could see that you were disdainful of the pettiness and internal machinations of an army. He said an army is not always a moral entity. You could not accept the immorality of slavery as a cause for which to fight."

Settle paused for a moment, then he began, "I had built my case on the solidarity of the Union at all costs. With Lincoln's final provocation, I was caught up in the furor of patriotism. As long as I was convinced that ours was a defense of our rights, our freedoms, I was willing to take my stand. I do not claim that I was somehow duped but I do believe now that many were.

"The cause of the South, now, is clearly slavery - its perpetuation. The secessionists, however, had so skillfully clad it in the right of states to secede, that the powder was set, the ball was placed, and Lincoln provided the lit fuse. I surveyed my men and I saw few who owned slaves and a few more that owned only one or two. The leadership of the Confederacy was made up of slave owners. I was part of that leadership and I had allowed myself to be compromised into defense of a practice that I despised as immoral. I admit to acting out of some level of petty pique at the time of my resignation, but I am now at peace with my decision. I grieve because others have to suffer."

The Doctor had listened quietly because he understood that Tom needed to say these things to him, that he was venting his own turmoil. 'Weren't we all?' he responded.

E.T. struggled for an answer. "I can appreciate the depth of your emotion, Thomas, but I cannot hide my ambivalence."

"Ambivalence!" cried Settle. "How can we equate slavery to ambivalence?"

"Hold a moment."

Settle realized he had reacted too harshly in the man's own home. "I am sorry."

"No, do not apologize. Too long have we talked in riddles and covered with platitudes. Half of my wealth is in my slaves. Without labor, I cannot produce crops. Labor drives my economy. All those forces struggle with the morality of slavery in a democracy. The fox chases his tail."

Enoch heard most of this conversation in segments as he passed in and out of the room, bringing trays of drinks, retrieving empty glasses, and clearing crumbs. He, like the other house slaves, functioned in a realm of consciousness that seemed to suspend through the functioning of the master's house. They were no part of the words that were spoken but they heard most of it and were adept at committing words to memory. The accumulation of his impressions would spread through the quarters that evening.

The slaves were deeply concerned about the debate over slavery. The owners were obviously being forced toward decisions not entirely of their own making. In hearing, without input, it was hard to interpret good or bad, right or wrong, but they knew it was their circumstances being debated and they could only observe. There were no plans or preparations to be made - only listen, observe.

Chapter 5

Settle sought no place in state government under the Confederacy but in the first election following war's end, he was sent to the North Carolina Senate where he was chosen by the members as Speaker. As an example of how diverse political opinion was at this moment, Unionists had not all been opposed to slavery and some who had been loyal to the Union felt that the Emancipation should not reasonably apply to them. Party affiliations were thus finding new formats. Settle, a pre-war Democrat, would follow his Unionist sympathies and opposition to slavery, into the new party affiliation. The animosity cultivated in a war, naturally carried over into the politics of Reconstruction.

As the war entered 1864, a strong Peace Party had risen and Settle was a member. His friend from Chapel Hill, Zebulon B. Vance, was campaigning for re-election as Governor. William W. Holden, like Settle a former Democrat, was his opponent. The prospect of defeat had led to increased levels of bitterness and frustration.

In the circle of campaigning throughout the state, Vance had reached Wentworth where Settle was prepared to debate him in support of Holden. The previous day, Vance had been in Madison and he asked Settle to postpone the debate, in response to his Madison remarks for a day, as he was fatigued. Settle agreed on the assurance that Vance would make no inflammatory statements to the local crowds.

They were both accommodated at the Wright Tavern, across from the courthouse, which was the only local hotel. The Governor was given a room in the Tavern building while Settle had one of a string of rooms that had been added to the west side of the Tavern, referred to locally as the 'upper hotel'.

The Union majority in Rockingham County had been broken at the outset of fighting and what was referred to now as the 'war-element' placed the Conservatives in the majority. The most combative of that group was fortified with whiskey and threats that had been made at Madison, became bolder as the day went on in Wentworth. Bellicose language had become the stuff of politics.

Settle's room was on the ground floor and fronted on a small yard about ten feet from the fence at the street. That fence ran about two hundred feet toward the public square around the courthouse. Settle was studying quietly in his room when a very large man appeared in the doorway cursing him as a traitor. The judge ordered him away but saw that the yard was now filled with an excited mob.

"It is a public hotel and I have as much right to be here as do the likes of you," said the man.

"This is my room. Please leave!"

"You coward. The likes of you have no place in this country."

With that, Settle clenched his fist and struck the man. The crowd surged forward and a dozen hands reached out to take hold of Tom. At that moment, Settle saw a silver-plated pistol rise forward above his left shoulder pointed directly at the crowd. In the nervous grasp of his brother, David Settle, it swept the mob. Every hand dropped and they fell back. Although their opinions in politics had never agreed, David had shared Tom's choice to leave the army in 1862.

Cowed by David Settle's quick action, the crowd reverted to a general brawl with a newly arrived element, about thirty-five members of Judge Settle's old Company I. They happened at the time to be home on furlough and saw the threat to their former commander. In moments, every fence picket had been wrenched off as a weapon. The mob was put to flight.

Scattering around Wentworth, opposing groups took up the quarrel and there was a general turmoil. Governor Vance had seen the fighting and took the opportunity to ask Settle to come to his room. They sat calmly chatting until the noise again seemed to approach the hotel. Settle declared that he could not hide from his friends in difficulty. Vance tried to hold him back and stood in the doorway. Settle simply lifted the larger man aside and joined his friends in the fight.

Among the first that he saw outside was the large man who had originally accosted him at his room. "I am going to kick you out of this town," declared Settle and proceeded to repeatedly kick the man who retreated toward his buggy and was driven away. The man is reported to have become subsequently Settle's fast friend and supporter.

On June 22, 1867, Thomas Settle made what came to be remembered as his seminal speech concerning his views on slavery and of future racial relationships. It was at Spring Garden an old muster ground for the Militia between Madison and Leaksville. A platform was set in the center and crowds arrived on foot and wagons and buggies were drawn up in a circle. A small band and introductory speeches warmed the audience. This was the core of plantation country in the Dan Valley. The audience was mixed. Unlike before the war, the former slaves did not hang back at the fringes but were scattered up to the base of the platform. Settle was introduced with much fanfare and acknowledged the cheers.

"Thank you! Thank you! Many of the neighbors and friends, especially among the colored people, have expressed a desire to hear my views on public affairs. I am here today to comply with that request, and I am glad to see both races represented in my audience for I have no arguments for the one that cannot be properly addressed to the other. Your rights and duties are mutual and the sooner you understand them, the better for both.

"This is a novel scene in Rockingham. You who were lately slaves, and you who but lately owned them, are here today equals before the law, inquiring as to the best policy for governing your common country. How has all this happened? It is the result of certain causes that were intended to produce an entirely different state of things. The politicians of the cotton states had for a long time contended that cotton was king, and if they could divide the Union and separate the Southern from the Northern States, they could build up the richest and most powerful government on earth, upon the foundation of slavery. In 1860 and 1861 they had succeeded 'in firing the Southern heart" to an extent that enabled them to 'precipitate a revolution' which has worked out results a little different from their program. In the first place, we did not exactly get out of the Union, though I confess it is somewhat difficult to find precisely where we are. Of one thing that I am certain, some of us are trying to get back. In the next place, instead of perpetuating and extending slavery, it is dead forever, and our black neighbors are here today with more powers and privileges than your most zealous and sanguine friends ever expected to be able to confer upon them."

Someone from the crowd called, "Mister Settle. I am bound to remind you that this war was about the rights of sovereign states to leave the Union in peace."

Settle reviewed his opinion that the rights of states to withdraw from the Union had only screened the real cause as preservation of slavery.

Then he went on. "For whatever may have been said in other days, it will hardly be pretended, in the light of the present events, the freeman, animated by all the hopes of life, and knowing that their wives and children will enjoy the proceeds of their labor will now develop the resources of a country faster than slaves who have no objects or aims in life, and no incentive to labor save fear. If any portion of my audience has not surrendered old prejudices on this subject, let me inquire of them, why have the Northern States, with a poorer soil and a cooler climate (all their disadvantages of soil and climate) so far surpassed their Southern sisters? Why do the bleak and barren hills of New England bloom like gardens, while your fertile and sunny slopes are covered with broom sedge, and are commonly and properly described as 'old fields?' Why do churches, school houses, railroads, canals, steam boats, factories, workshops, cities, towns, beautiful villages and neat farm houses exist and flourish there, while poverty and pride constitute our fortune here? The one is the result of free labor, the other of slavery, which has been a blight and mildew upon every land it has ever touched.

"My land ain't blighted and there ain't no mildew on me," came from the audience.

Settle took on the need to purge bitterness and bind up the social wounds from war.

"There is no reason why the two races should be at enmity but many good reasons why they should be friends; our common interests demand it, and I trust our hearts feel it. Surely slave owners can entertain no unworthy prejudice against a people who remained with them faithfully to the last, and forebore to participate in a struggle which, after 1863, was avowedly for their freedom. After that period they knew that one army was fighting for freedom and the other for slavery; and yet they remained faithful, kind and obedient too, protecting and feeding the families of those who were trying to perpetuate their bondage. Here again in this remarkable contest we see conduct so contrary to the promptings of human feelings, but we are constrained to believe that a merciful providence was guiding the whole matter, with a wisdom above the reach of man. Then let us be friends and work together for our mutual advantage.

"My advice to the white man is to be kind and just to the colored man, make fair and liberal contracts with him, and stand up for them even to your hurt, and it is precisely the same to the colored man. Heretofore the black man has had but little opportunity to form a general character; it will not be so hereafter. The broad world is now before you, and you will soon make some form of a mark upon it. Your general bearing and your dealings with men will soon make for you a general character. You can make it good, bad, or indifferent, just as you see proper.

"It is right and proper that we should all remember that slavery is a national sin. The North is as much responsible for its introduction here as the South. They had the good sense to get rid of it, while the South was foolish enough to try to perpetuate it; but so far as the sin and social evil are concerned, both are equally guilty.

"I am at least in a position to give you disinterested advice. I do not know that I have pleased anybody. True, I have an interest in this extent. This is the land of my birth. I do not propose to leave it. My home is here, my grave will be here. My children are here, and I wish them a government fit to live in. The object of my admonition now is to see the country developed. I have witnessed the first great step. I have seen freedom take the place of slavery."

Settle knew he was being a little disingenuous to claim disinterest but he was attempting to present himself as the bridging voice of reconstruction. What he presented for the people of Rockingham in that Spring Garden speech was a road to reconciliation. He recognized that former slaves would need the active exertion of the white community in order to institute even the general character required to assume a partnership in community. Instead, Conservative politicians found it more attractive to resort to obstructionist tactics that pitted race against race. Maneuvering the franchise to minimize the impact of black suffrage over the next few years, reclaimed their control of state politics for much of the next century. The Spring Garden speech was also made at the time that Settle was one of the founders of the Republican Party in North Carolina and his views can be said to have been an expression of that party's position on slavery and race relations.

In 1868, Settle was appointed a Justice of the North Carolina Supreme Court. Holden had now been elected Governor. It was the period of repeated violent action by the Ku Klux Klan. In Rockingham a black woman was killed by a shot through her own front door. In another case, chunks of lit firewood were thrust into the faces and mouths of victims. Houses were torched in Madison belonging to white families seen to sympathize with blacks. In Caswell County, the Kirk-Holden War resulted in the call out first of detectives and then militia.

On at least two occasions different Klans made specific plans to assassinate Settle. One design was directed at Settle and the covered bridge, built over the Dan near his plantation, that was despised by his enemies. It was agreed that he would be taken captive on the road and tied to the

134

bridge which would then be set afire. Only the presence among the hooded Klan of a friend, gave the plan away.

Public political meetings frequently resulted in brawls and fist fights. Settle took to arming himself with a knife strapped under his pant leg at his ankle, a pair of pistols in his vest pockets, or a six-shooter behind his back.

His reputation was growing nationally even as it was embattled in North Carolina. In early June 1872 he presided over the Republican National Convention in Philadelphia where President Ulysses S. Grant was nominated for a second term.

In 1876, the Centennial Year, in North Carolina the Conservatives had adopted the name Democrat and nominated former war-Governor, Zebulon B. Vance. The Republicans chose Thomas Settle. The campaign came to be known as the 'Battle of Giants' with vigorous debates in cities across the state. Settle was defeated by less than 14000 votes out of 233,000 cast. The Democrats claimed the state had been redeemed, home rule restored, and white supremacy established.

In 1877, Federal troops were withdrawn from North Carolina. The Legislature passed restrictive suffrage laws disenfranchising much of the black vote. A decade later, Alfred Moore Scales was elected 45th Governor of the state as a Democrat.

BOOK VI
IMPEACHMENT

Chapter 1

Robert Martin Douglas was only eighteen when he received his under-graduate degree from Georgetown in 1867. The year before his step-mother had remarried and it was time to make his own way.   The will of his grandmother in 1860 had left him, individually, her 900 acre dower interests in the Robert Martin estate in North Carolina and it divided the remaining value including the slaves with his brother, Stephen.   He and Stevie jointly owned all the interests of their mother in North Carolina and Mississippi and their interest in their father's estate in Illinois. It seemed logical that Robert would return to Rockingham County, where he had spent so much of the good years of his childhood including the visits to his mother's grave. His grandmother had demonstrated her particular interest in him and her plantation had gone through the Civil War and Emancipation and now was in need of attention.   There was further encouragement that the plantation had given the name Douglas to the surrounding area and a US Post Office, so it seemed appropriate that a son of the Great Orator should be in residence.

Much of the furniture at Douglas had come from Robert's great uncle, Governor Alexander Martin and his great, great grandmother, Jane Hunter Martin, from Danbury Plantation. One of the slaves, Billy Jesse, was grandson of Prince, whom Governor Martin had freed in 1807 for "the many faithful & meritorious services the said Prince has rendered me in my life time." The children of

Prince were not given the freedom of their father so Billy Jesse had been a slave until he was emancipated.

Robert's arrival back in Rockingham County coincided with the rise of violence and intimidation of incorrigible whites and the spread of secret night-riding organizations that came to be called collectively the Ku Klux Klan. The rise of the Klan had been gradual and Governor William Holden appealed to the great majority of peace abiding North Carolinians to reject these excesses but with little success. He realized that a more sustained effort was going to be necessary.

It was at this time that he asked Robert Martin Douglas. son of the man he had originally supported in that pivotal election of 1860, to be his private secretary. Robert had all the obvious historical connections with the roots of the Republican Party. He had just completed his education in Washington, DC. He represented new blood but also connected blood within the party.

"Robert, you are the new generation," Holden told the young man. "We all come from the generation of compromise and the people of bloodshed. In the midst of the late war, your Uncle, Thomas Settle, acting as my stand in during my campaign against Vance for Governor, was nearly killed in Wentworth just a few miles from your plantation. You represent the people who will rebuild the Union for which your father dedicated his life. Your family is truly in North Carolina, the most accepted defenders of the cause for which Lincoln died. I need that public image."

MARTIN-SETTLE

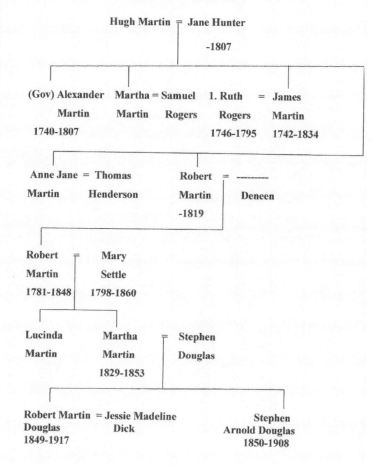

Hugh Martin = Jane Hunter

-1807

(Gov) Alexander   Martha = Samuel   1. Ruth   = James
Martin   Martin   Rogers   Rogers   Martin
1740-1807   1746-1795 1742-1834

Anne Jane = Thomas   Robert   = ---------
Martin   Henderson   Martin   Deneen
                      -1819

Robert = Mary
Martin   Settle
1781-1848 1798-1860

Lucinda   Martha = Stephen
Martin   Martin   Douglas
             1829-1853

Robert Martin = Jessie Madeline   Stephen
Douglas   Dick   Arnold Douglas
1849-1917   1850-1908

Not lost on Holden was the fact that two of the most recalcitrant counties in the state, hotbeds of the Klan, were Caswell and Alamance along the eastern borders of Rockingham and Guilford Counties. From July of 1868, Robert had influence on Holden's efforts to rally the state against the excesses of the Klan.

In March General Ulysses S. Grant was elected President as a Republican against New York Governor Horatio Seymour. He pressed forward to complete the promise of Reconstruction. In April Robert was in Washington and he went to present his compliments to Grant upon his election. As a child, Robert had known Grant as a neighbor. The conversation was a reunion and Grant was interested in the job Martin had accepted with Governor Holden. He offered him the post as his assistant private secretary. Robert returned to North Carolina, advised the Governor of his good fortune and arranged for the management of his Dan River plantation. Seven months later, he was promoted to private secretary of the President of the United States.

Robert M. Douglas' political worlds were playing out simultaneously in Washington and North Carolina. In the latter, Governor Holden was attempting to maintain authority over a situation rapidly spiraling out of hand. Among other excesses in the state, Wyatt Outlaw, leader of the black Republicans in Alamance County, was lynched on the court house square in Graham. Then State Senator John W. "Chicken" Stephens of Caswell County was murdered by the Klan inside the court house in Yanceyville.

141

Holden received approval from President Grant and support with equipment and the offer of men, to organize a regiment of Unionists in the state under the command of George W. Kirk. Kirk was from western North Carolina and his troops came mainly from the western counties. With the troops mustered and on the move, Holden went to Washington and met with Grant and Douglas was present. Federal Troops were quartered still throughout the southern states. Grant reaffirmed his support for Holden's action and again said he was ready to provide more direct support if necessary.

"Kirk's War" in Caswell and Alamance succeeded in breaking the power of the Klan but the entire incident led to the Impeachment of the Governor and his conviction by the Legislature. Douglas could be a kind of "point man" for the President, during all this period, for the volatile situation in North Carolina.

The late Senator John "Chicken" Stephens grew up in Wentworth in a house adjacent to the court house. His political foes had preserved the rumor that as a young man he had stolen some chickens and hence his nickname. The house was immediately across the street from Wright Tavern, the point of the near assassination of Thomas Settle in 1864.

Robert Martin Douglas served as the private secretary for the President for most of Grant's first term. In that period Grant enforced civil rights laws, prosecuted the Ku Klux Klan and passed the 15th Amendment to the Constitution which guaranteed the right of every citizen to

142

vote regardless of their "race, creed, or previous condition of servitude."

Chapter 2

It was probably Thomas Settle who first mentioned to David Settle Reid that their cousins, Robert Martin Douglas and Josiah Thomas Settle, were now in Washington. Reid, ever the matchmaker, seems to have advised both young men and advised them of their proximity. It promised an interesting interaction as Douglas, Grant's private secretary and a recent graduate of Georgetown, and Settle, his Negro cousin who was at Howard University and working for the Freedmen's Bureau in the War Department. The young men had never met but were well aware of their relationship.

The first meeting occurred at the Freedmen's Bureau where Settle, younger by a year, was pleased to introduce his cousin, the President's private secretary. Both young men were heady with achievement and conscious of the symbolism of their lives, in their family, in their environment, in tumultuous times.

"Robert, welcome to the Freedmen's Bureau. Though we have not met, I feel I have known you all my life," began Settle.

"Let us start by agreeing to call each other Bob and Joe. I think I am correct in understanding that you prefer that to Josiah."

"Done!"

What followed was a torrent, let loose as if for years it had been held back somewhere waiting for an eventual convergence.

"When Cousin David advised me of your whereabouts in Washington, I could not wait for this moment," said Bob. "Let me understand our setting, family-wise. You and I are but a year apart. You and my late mother, however, were first cousins which I believe, makes us first cousins once removed."

"Yes, a bit out of sequence because I came late in life for my parents and your mother died when I was just three."

They talked family for a while and then it was Joe who seemed to want to first break the racial ice. There was so much to say and this seemed like a fortuitous place for the dialogue.

"What a place and time for us to meet! My mother was a slave, daughter of a white man, and married to your white Great Uncle. Your mother was married to the tireless defender of the Union and opponent of slavery, Senator Stephen A. Douglas. Here we are in the Freedmen's Bureau."

"It does drip with symbolism, doesn't it. I have got to hear from you the story of the progress of your family after they left North Carolina."

Joe paused and then began to outline what he remembered of the experience of his family. Then he posed to Bob, the question that had frequently concerned him. "What was the talk in North Carolina, about us, the black branch - the children of the slave and Uncle Josiah?"

"You were always thought of as 'the family," said Bob. "It was a puzzlement to us as children. We wondered what you did during the war. It was like an intrigue, I

145

guess. But there was never any denial or effort that I saw, to pretend that you and your family did not exist. You were in Ohio and we were in North Carolina and there was little likelihood I presume that we would meet. You know, when I most remember a discussion about you and your family was with my grandmother, Mary Martin. You may not know, but my brother and I spent a lot of time in our youth with our grandmother Martin. We had a step-mother who was good to us and our father was very busy. We would come mostly in the summer and grandmother would arrange to take us to the family cemetery."

"I've heard about that place and always dreamed what it must have been like."

"It was not very different from those family graveyards that dotted the plantations along the Dan River. What was always a wonder for us, was the big box tombs of our grandfather, our mother and our Aunt Lucinda, lined in a row at the top of the hill. Stevie and I used to pretend that they were all in those marble boxes on top of the grave but grandmother assured that they were buried below. We had picnics and we talked about the family and that is where I got most of my understanding about the family. One other stone was a special curiosity for us. It was for Washington who we were told was your oldest brother."

"Oh yes, Washington," Joe mused. "As children we were told that he was killed in an accident but mother always shut down any discussion."

"Grandmother described a Christmas Day," said Bob, "when Washington was allowed to go hunting with his father and some other men. I think she said he was

146

sixteen. He was running with a shotgun and tripped. As he fell, the gun went off and he was killed. There was a large white stone at his grave with part of the story all written out. On the other side of the box graves, was a smaller stone for Frances Graves Settle, your father's first wife." Bob paused thinking for a moment that it had been unkind to mention Josiah Settle's first wife.

"We knew about her and that we had two white step-sisters who were married and lived in Georgia. I don't know that my father and mother ever heard much from them."

"Alright! So we got here. To the nation's capital after a Civil War and after all the slaves were free. Of course I considered Washington also was my home. My step-mother had seen to it that we were brought up Catholic, which was her religion. My education at Georgetown was almost foreordained. The school was just down the road. I got my degree in '67."

"That was the year that Howard University was established. I started my college education at Oberlin, a small liberal arts college in Ohio that had been admitting Negroes for some years. It had been a hotbed of Abolitionists and was a stop on the Underground Railroad. There were only four of us Negroes but I got along well in my freshman year. Then my father died. He had been for some reason very anxious for me to get the best education possible. My other brothers and sisters had only limited schooling. We had heard that a new college was being started in Washington connected with the Freedmen's

147

Bureau, just for Negroes and as a sophomore I got into the first class. So that is how I got here."

Chapter 3

There were a lot of meetings between the cousins over a four year period. They kept up with the difficulties of Bob's former boss, Governor Holden and Kirk's War against the KKK. They followed closely the passage of the 15th Amendment. Bob and Joe were a conduit for the President about the work of the Freedmen's Bureau.

One evening they were in Joe's room at Howard having attended a play at the school. They were both keenly aware of themselves in this place. Joe seemed to want to speak more insightfully than they had yet been able to, comfortably. Maybe he felt he was more secure on his own turf.

"Bob, you and I share a common descent, common blood, but through my mother I have different blood, black blood. In this country that makes you the "we" and me the "they".

Bob was a little startled but waited for Joe to fill out his thesis. "Negro, black, slave, they are all part of how we have dealt with race in America. My African ancestors were brought out of that continent to the Western Hemisphere. In places like South America, Cuba, the Dominican Republic, Africans were another ethnic group, like Spanish or Portuguese, not indigenous. In the North American mainland colonies, the practice became to treat Africans as a different race. In order to more narrowly define the difference, it became a single drop of blood that constituted the line. Black was an obvious difference but where that dissimilarity was not so obvious, the measure of the presence of one drop of black blood made a Negro and all blacks were automatically slaves. This wasn't true at first. At Jamestown the ethnic model prevailed.

"Anyhow, over time, one drop of black blood became the definer and therefore the child of a female slave was automatically a slave as was a black child born to a white woman. When in doubt, that single drop of blood defined a slave."

"Of course a slave could be freed by law and at the request of the owner," noted Bob.

"True, but even they were then known as a free black and thus stereotyped in society. The point is that race, race, race, became the basis upon which the American society developed. The 'we and they' of the class evolved and it was convenient, and it was encapsulated in law, and it became justified by faith.

"When the founders came to define the terms of the declaration that they were making as free people, 'We, the people,' was only a room full of old, white men. If there was a we, there had to be a they. We was not women. It was not American Indians and it could certainly not be slaves. And so the legal structure of our laws evolved into the United States of America. Oh, the one drop rule gave us problems. If seats in legislatures were based on population, how would the slave population be counted? Some states did not want slavery so as new states joined the union, could they choose to be slave or non-slave? If they could, then how could we maintain the balance of voting majorities on the issue? Bob, it is a history, a lesson in civics but let me tell you that this history is what makes you white and me black in America. Lincoln understood that the Civil War had to end slavery in the 14th amendment once and for all. He also understood that the end of slavery was not the end of the separation of race."

"I have had similar discussions with President Grant. He pushed for the 15th amendment understanding that those whom the nation freed had to have full rights of suffrage. It is a process, Joe."

"Easy for you to say. It is my process, not yours. I don't mean to sound harsh but Negroes are still the they of this society."

"I guess the metaphor then exists in the 'We, the people.' The founders knew full well the imperfections in the claim they were making. They could only finally set a standard to which they intended the new country would aspire. You and I find ourselves in the midst of precipitous change. We are the human contradiction of the division by race. It seems to me that gives us a particular empathy that we are obliged to utilize in our lifetime to advance the process.

"Do we not sound noble? Brothers. Cousins but in a nation yet divided against itself. I am aware of our youth, Bob. I am also aware that I am the exceptional ex-slave. I have the liberation of education and I can walk and strut my exceptionalism or I can reach back to the poorest, blackest ex-slave in Mississippi and give them a hand. Is there really a choice?"

On that evening Robert Douglas and Josiah Settle had defined the course that their lives would take.

On another occasion Bob expressed to Joe his concern that he had not yet been able to attend Law School. "Poor Bob," chided Joe. "He has to be the private secretary of the President of the United States and he doesn't have time to go to law school. What a disappointment."

"Oh, you know what I mean. I know what a golden opportunity I have but at some point, I need to get along with the basics of my career."

"It is funny how opportunity matches timing. I am finishing at Howard just when they have decided to start their Law School and I can keep all my jobs and move right into the first class. Of course, we are meeting in upper rooms and faculty homes but I will be part of the first class. You'll get your chance."

They followed carefully the impeachment of Governor William Holden. Grant was very perplexed. The first issue of the debate over impeachment, concluded in Holden's favor, determined that the insurrection in North Carolina had been against the government of the United States. Holden thus had the right to move against the Klan in Caswell and Alamance. The second point, the charge that the Governor did not have the right to the supposed unlawful arrests and detentions of suspects he had made during the insurrection, was defined more sharply.

When Holden saw popular opinion and the votes in the Legislature swinging against him, he went to Washington. Again Douglas was part of the deliberations and Holden had the full backing of the President. As he lobbied Capitol Hill, Congress received a message from Grant requesting "sever laws to put down the Ku Klux

152

Klan." The national Republicans were effusively praising Holden claiming he had "saved the country in 1872, and from a terrible civil war." It was not enough to save Holden in North Carolina and he was removed from office. .

At the end, Holden remained in Washington seeking a government position. He was not the only one seeking patronage. Grant's young secretary, Robert M. Douglas received appointment as U.S. Marshall for the newly created Western District of North Carolina of the United States Circuit Court. This was the same sympathetic western district from which Holden had pulled his state forces under George Kirk to go against the Klan. The appointment was a political plumb.

Returning to North Carolina, Douglas settled in Greensboro and on June 24, 1874 he married Jessie Madeline Dick, daughter of Robert Paine Dick, formerly a justice of the North Carolina Supreme Court and currently a United States District Court Judge.

Judge Dick was not only Douglas' political ally. He also agreed with his determination to become an attorney. It just so happened that Dick and his law partner, John H. Dillard, both with roots in Rockingham County and both close friends of the Settles and the Reids, operated Greensboro Law School in downtown Greensboro. By 1885, Bob had completed his studies and passed the bar. He was appointed Standing Master of Chancery of the Western District of the United States Circuit Court where he had previously been Marshall

Chapter 4

Bob became a member of the Guilford County Bar at a time when it included many of the lawyer/gladiators who had struggled with the causes of Union and Secession. Now these same men were defining the structure of the Republican and Democratic Parties in the state, the former newly made and the latter reconstituted. The Republicans viewed the newly enfranchised Negro as the potential constituency that could help them control the South. The Democrats had determined to appeal to all the poor farmers and unreconstructed Rebels, who saw the Negro as a threat or image of their defeat, as their constituency that could deliver a majority.

John A. Gilmer, brothers Alfred M. and Junius I. Scales, Ralph Gorrell, Cyrus P. Mendenhall, Frank Caldwell, and John M. Morehead were powerful Democrats and Thomas Keogh, William Scott, Albion Tourgée, and R.P. Dick were equally powerful Republicans in Guilford. Gilmer formed a partnership with Thomas Ruffin, jr., and John H. Dillard, and the latter two were judges of the state Supreme Court. Dillard and Dick were not training Democrats or Republicans but Attorneys in their Greensboro Law School.

Organized violence became commonplace and was directed mostly at the Republicans. During the decade of the 1870s the parties were nearly equally balanced in Guilford. By 1888, when Douglas had become master

Greensboro's State Supreme Court Associate Justices. *Upper left*, Judge Robert Paine Dick. *Upper right*, Judge Thomas Settle, Jr. *Lower left*, Judge John Henry Dillard. *Lower right*, Judge Robert Martin Douglas.

Courtesy of Ethel Stephens Arnett

In Chancery of the district, the Republicans were in power. Of course, their national control of the executive gave them significant patronage power and in many Southern states enhanced their competitive position.

In the 1876 election when Unionist Thomas Settle, Robert Douglas' great uncle, fought the Gubernatorial "Battle of Giants" with Zebulon B. Vance, the winning Democrats claimed that they had 'redeemed' the state from the threat of Negro rule. For a decade, Democrats controlled state government.

That control came under risk with the economic depression of the 1880s and the economic burden of the time fell hardest on the small farmers and tenant farmers. They began to care less about their fear of Negro dominance and to suspect more that the Democrats were no longer their friend. A populist movement nationally became the Populist Party led by North Carolinian, Leonidas Polk.

Just before the election of 1894, the Populists and the Republicans formed a fusion partnership and carried the election in the state. They immediately enacted a series of reforms including a liberalized election law that made it easier to vote and increased registered voters by 80,000, partly by color coding the parties on the ballot to allow illiterates to have a political voice.

Robert Douglas was nominated for the North Carolina Supreme Court in 1897 on the Republican-Populist fusion ticket. Although the state court system was populated throughout this period by a high caliber of jurists, most came to power, or eventually lost office, through the degree of patron's influence within the parties.

Douglas was considered a judge of outstanding learning, fairness, patience, and impartiality. William P. Bynum, another noted jurist said, "His written opinions display not only a thorough comprehension of fundamental legal principles, but an ornateness of style and lucidity of expression which have never been excelled by any member of the court."

The fusion policy of Republicans and Populists held through several election cycles before the Democrats decided to focus their campaign in 1898 on the single issue of white supremacy. What had been benign now became blatant, the fear of Negro domination. The Democrats threatened violence reverting to some of the 'red shirt' tactics of "Pitchfork' Ben Tillman in South Carolina.

Regaining control of the electorate, the Democrats passed legislation that effectively disenfranchised Negroes for generations to come. After the Fusion Governor Daniel Russell left office in 1900, North Carolina Republicans did not regain the office of Governor until 1972.

The redemption that the Democrats provided to correct the "excesses" they claimed fusion had given to North Carolina, amounted to petty politics. While fusion had sought to increase the body politic, and improve the lot of the poor farmer, many of whom were black, the resurgent Democrats saw to it that the penitentiary system was rehabilitated. They protected the special interests of such eastern establishments as the oyster industry, and on the pretext of mismanagement, they appointed competing boards and commissions in order to take over the functioning power of the state agencies.

The legislature ousted from office, Republicans and Populists by creating new offices with the same duties, then unfunding the former office. Many of these conflicting office cases began appearing before the state supreme court in the form of mandamus cases. Initially the court, using a 1833 NC Supreme Court decision in *Hoke vs Henderson,* decided unanimously that a man appointed or elected to public office had an estate, or property right in his office. Therefore the Legislature could not destroy the office and thus eliminate the estate.

By the end of the century North Carolina was the only state holding to this right of estate and opinion in the state was shifting. The Legislature, in the hands of the Democrats, began to reduce Republicans in appointed office by renaming the office, appointing Democrats to the office, and ceasing to pay the former office holder. The Supreme Court held in several cases against the Legislation based on *Hoke,* directing that the office holder should be paid.

On the pretext that the court had no right of mandamus, the Democrats sought to remove the Republican members of the state supreme court and brought impeachment proceedings for high crimes and misdemeanors against David M. Furches and Robert M. Douglas. Five separate counts were read out against the Justices on February 25, 1901.

The Legislature, fearing they might be doing wrong to good men, made assurance that they never intended to charge Fuches and Douglas "with the slightest personal interest in these matters nor was there the slightest taint of personal corruption." It was still charged that "they did an act forbidden by law. They sinned against light and knowledge."

Justice Walter A. Montgomery, democrat, charged his fellow Justice, Walter Clark, "Your dissenting opinions relative to these office holding cases have been so full of political leaning that I cannot hear to it. You have been at the bottom of the trouble the Court has had along these lines. The newspaper attacks have come from you and I know it." In the end the vote was 27 guilty, 23 not guilty: short of the 2/3 vote required to convict. On all counts, the justices were acquitted.

Unlike his former boss, Governor William W. Holden, Douglas survived the impeachment efforts of his enemies He completed his eight years on the state supreme court but in 1908 he refused to entertain nomination for re-election to the office. He returned to Greensboro to practice law. He was an organizer of the Greensboro Chamber of Commerce, a director of the Greensboro Loan and Trust Company and was an active member of the Guilford Battleground Company.

BOOK VII
Joe

Chapter 1

"You are the son of our Exodus, Joe," Josiah Settle said to his boy. "There was so much symbolism about your arrival. Your mother and I had no children after Washington's death. We had finally made the decision to leave North Carolina and my family. Then your mother became pregnant and I wanted to wait until the following year. She insisted we hold with our plan and you were delivered in route. You were born on our way to a new beginning that we had hoped would offer more opportunity for our children. You seemed to be a promise."

"Yes, Papa but you did not find what you sought in Mississippi."

"No. That is true. I should have known but I was so anxious to take advantage of the boom in cotton plantations that I deceived myself and your mother."

"But you were able to finally free us from slavery."

"Yes, but that also meant that you could not stay in Mississippi."

"We are all free and you and Mama have been able to marry in Ohio. We are happy here. Why is it that you and Mama live apart?"

"There is not a single answer, Joe. Even in Ohio,, our mixed marriage was not accepted by everyone. People were nice enough to our faces but some did not approve. For more than twenty years we had essentially lived apart in North Carolina and we were accustomed to the circumstances of a single household, except briefly in Mississippi. I guess we figured that we were really accustomed to that life style and if it helped mollify our neighbors, we would do so in Ohio."

"You know, to us as children, we saw it as fun to go back and forth as we pleased. I know all the older boys were happy not to have us little ones running around. Most of the time, we ate together. We all had to get used to attending school and for a while, for some of us, we had to catch up with the children of our age. I was lucky. As the next youngest, I first started school after we got to Ohio."

Ohio law said that where separate schools were not provided black children had to be accepted in the white schools. There were few other blacks so the Settle children went to the white schools. They were not used to school anyway but to enter school under such latent hostility required them to struggle for a place.

Joe was fortunate when a liberal white teacher took charge of the school and took a special interest in him. He found an equal attachment to the teacher and he was soon excelling. She was the one who began to inspire him to something more than a country schoolhouse education. Josiah was pleased to encourage such a course of study for Joe.

In 1866, Joe was sent to Oberlin, Ohio where he was prepared for two years to enter the college. Oberlin was the first college in the United States to regularly admit Negroes in 1836. Although he was one of four blacks in an entering class of almost fifty, he was chosen to be one of the eight class orators.

He had completed his freshman year when Josiah Settle suddenly died in 1869. This made for an uncertain financial situation and Nancy was not as eager as had been Josiah, for Joe to leave. Joe convinced her that he should transfer to Howard University in Washington, DC anticipating that he might expect to make contacts that could lead to government jobs. Howard had been chartered at the end of the Civil War and was closely connected to the Freedman's Bureau. Joe was able to get a job as a clerk in the Education Division of the Bureau.

One of the goals at Howard was to offer opportunities for Negro youth to find work in government and to involve themselves in politics. Joe was enthusiastic about politics and willing to do what was necessary to enter party politics.

He graduated with the first college graduating class at Howard in 1872. At the time of his graduation he was acting as Reading Clerk of the DC House of Delegates, teaching Latin and one class in mathematics at the University, and pursuing his own coursework. He had immediately upon graduation, entered the Law school at Howard and graduated three years later.

Chapter 2

As a student, Joe had been active in political canvassing and fund raising. He was employed by several boards and committees of the District of Columbia.

During the presidential campaign of 1872, he canvassed in Maryland and Virginia in the interest of the Republicans. He even went home to Ohio and made speeches for the ticket in Hamilton, Dayton, and Cleveland.

Upon graduation, he was elected to the bar of the Supreme Court in DC. He had, however, decided, through his experience with the work of the Freedmen's Bureau, to return to the south to practice law. In the spring of 1875 he located in Panola County, Mississippi. He returned that year to Washington and married Therese T. Vogelsang, niece of J. C. Bishop of Annapolis. She had been born in Albany, New York.

As Joe was almost immediately a force in the Republican Party in Mississippi, his first cousin, Thomas Settle, son of Uncle Thomas Settle, was Chairman of the 1872 Republican National Convention.

Four years later Joe was the Republican nominee for District Attorney for the 12th Circuit of Mississippi and Thomas Settle was the Republican nominee for Governor of North Carolina. When they met at the convention that year, it was as recognized leaders of the party in the South. Thomas was almost twenty years older.

"Joe, although we have not met before, I remember your father very well. Of course your older siblings are just my age and we grew up together," offered Tom as a beginning.

"You should know, Thomas, that part of my interest in Republican Party politics comes from hearing from afar about your contribution. I think it is fulfilling to be part of a political party so dedicated to the restoration of our country and making opportunity for all people."

Thomas was amused by the youthful enthusiasm of his cousin but he did not want to seem to doubt the party cause. "I have been in on the organization of the party in North Carolina from the beginning. Sometimes I think we Republicans are inclined to think that our cause rose like a phoenix out of the ashes of defeat. In reality, the period of the two decades, 1850s and 1860s, suffixed by a Civil War, was like a bitter metamorphous. In retrospect, I believe that was necessary as the only way this country could purge itself of the curse of slavery."

"I know that grandfather was a Democrat before the war but I always understood that was because of cousin David Settle Reid and Steven A. Douglas."

"That is essentially correct and I guess it makes the point I was striving for. Party labels are little more than big tents where as much diversity can be assembled as can be kept from murdering each other. Presumably, the bigger the tent, the more powerful the party. So don't fool yourself. We may wince when called Scalawag and Ccarpetbagger but we know there are such people among us. Former Whigs and Douglas Democrats and freedmen - we are a fractious group, Joe."

"You are surely correct. In Mississippi the struggle within the party between Governor Alcorn and Senator Adelbert Ames threatens to rip apart the party."

"I see this internecine struggle, coupled with the general racial animus pervading the South, as too much to contain within the party. Too many are Republicans because they saw it at the end of the Civil War as the winning party and were attracted by patronage. It is inevitable that soon Federal troops will be withdrawn from the South. When that happens, I fear that the Democrats will attract all that racial animus into a powerful majority."

"Do we have any recourse?"

"At this point, I think we can only hope to keep as much under that tent as possible. It makes for political tradeoffs and compromises and I am also afraid that the freedmen will be the biggest losers."

"It seems in many ways strange that we are able to speak so objectively, Tom. We are cousins. I was a slave and am now a freedman. You were a slave owner, a Confederate officer fighting in defense of slavery. Are all families so convoluted?"

"Ha! Indeed! I think we must be a fairly extreme case. But don't crucify me in being a soldier for the South. Early on, the cause of the South was illusive. When I came to realize that the price for defending my state was to be fighting to perpetuate slavery, I resigned and I was cursed as a consequence. I still like to say that I have been true to

Hon. J. T. Settle,
Memphis, Tenn.

Josiah Thomas Settle (1850-1900)

my moral sense as a Unionist recognizing that slavery was the national cancer since 1787 and it had to be removed."

Joe was mesmerized by his older cousin. Such a man would be able to make much progress as Governor. He knew though, that Thomas faced formidable opposition. At the same time he wanted to explore his opinion specifically concerning freedmen.

"Tom, you are perhaps aware that my law degree is from Howard and that I was immersed there in the activities of the Freedmen's Bureau. My white father had been a strong support for my education and he always talked of being educated to a purpose. I felt my purpose was to return to my native Mississippi to assist in the integration of former slaves into full participation in the government that was theirs."

"Joe, if I am not mistaken, you were born in Tennessee and I might note you were conceived in North Carolina. Could you not conclude that North Carolina was your native state?"

They both laughed. Tom continued. "I guess the question is a very fine point of when life begins. That will be a scientific question of the future that I am certain will be politicized."

"I thought when I was canvassing for the party here in Ohio in '72, that I might locate here but I came to the conclusion that I was more needed in the Deep South."

"You made a noble decision and it makes me hopeful for the future of the party and the nation. There will come a time, and I fear it will be soon, when the pendulum will swing away from progress back toward reaction. That will be the hardest on the freedmen because they will have the fewest defenders. They will be the easiest target. It will be the poor white, most amenable to political opportunists, who will vote to keep the Negro down. You will be in the eye of the hurricane."

The Republican Party lost heavily in 1875 in Mississippi. Joe lost in the 12th Circuit. The party was so badly defeated that they remained marginal for years.

1876 was the year that Thomas Settle was the Republican Candidate for Governor in North Carolina against Zebulon B. Vance in the "Battle of Giants." When Federal troops were removed from the South the next year, the Republican Party in North Carolina lost voters as laws were passed to block Black suffrage.

Josiah T. Settle's name was suggested for the Mississippi legislatures in 1883 but he held back. The next year he was nominated and elected, aided by a large Black community. Still he had to run as an Independent against the Fusion Party in order to be elected.

He was described then in the St. Louis Globe-Democrat as, "A colored orator - but the palm for natural ability as an orator - is borne by a colored man J. T. Settle, of Panola County. He comes of the famous North Carolina family of the name, is well-educated and a lawyer by profession. He is of spare figure, light of color and good looking. When he gets the floor he speaks in a manner to command the attention of the entire house."

He served only a single term and his defeat convinced him that he must concentrate on his law practice in the interest of his family. In 1885 he moved to Memphis, Tennessee.

Soon after his arrival, he was appointed Assistant Attorney General and at that time was considered a "master of elocution." He was noted as brilliant and "his manner was without ostentation as an honor to his profession."

That same year, his wife died leaving Joe without children. He was elected to the Republican State Executive Committee and in 1892 he was again a delegate to the Republican National Committee. Joe continued to believe that as a former slave, he should take part in politics in the best interest of his race.

"I no longer seek any public office cognizant as I am of the reality of the Republican Party here in Tennessee but I feel I can still be an effective voice for the Negro within the party. I am satisfied that my success as an attorney similarly brings respect and confidence to the character of the Negro."

In 1890 he married Fannie A. McCullough considered one of the most beautiful and accomplished women of Memphis. She was at the time of their marriage in charge of the musical department of LeMoyne Institute, a historically Black Educational Institute.

Joe and Fannie had two sons, Josiah T. Settle, Jr., and Francis McCullough Settle. He died in Memphis in 1915.

A Tennessee Highway Market has been erected honoring Josiah T. Settle near the river in Memphis. It notes "During the late 1880s, he served as Assistant Attorney General of the Criminal Court of Shelby County,

Tennessee Highway Marker-Memphis

Josiah Thomas Settle (1850-1915)

an appointment unprecedented for an African-American at that time."

Josiah T. Settle residence-Memphis, TN

BOOK VIII
NUBBIN RIDGE

Chapter 1

Could anyone find a more illusory name in the South than Nubbin Ridge? In North Carolina a highway historical marker locates it as the birthplace of Glenn T. Settle - three miles southeast. It is where a black and a white story come together and project a message.

It begins, as much of this story has, with Thomas Settle, a superior court judge in Rockingham County, North Carolina. His Antebellum plantation was a testimony to his wealth in rich red clay tobacco land. This is the same Thomas Settle whose twin sister, Mary, was married to Robert Martin and whose brother, Josiah, was the father of Josiah T. Settle.

This Thomas needed another field slave so he bought Tom from a Caswell County slave trader. Tom was a powerful specimen, obviously capable of performing the hard work in Settle's fields.

On the way home, after having made the purchase, Tom began to tell Settle a story.

"Back in Africa, I was a king."

"I have heard that story more than once from a black man. Were you King of Timbuktu?"

"No Master. I tell you true. See these marks?' He showed Settle designs on his body. "These are not scars. These are marks that every man from Africa know. They be when I become King and my father died."

Birthplace-Nubbin Ridge

REV. GLYNN T. SETTLE
ORIGINATOR
AND
DIRECTOR OF

Wings over Jordan

Wings Over Jordan Program

Then Tom went on to give details of places, an African tribe, and ceremonial details. He described the raiding party that came to his village and took him captive with ten others. They were kept in captivity until a slave ship came and they were sold to a slaver and Tom was brought to New Orleans. Settle could not investigate the truth of any of it but as Tom spoke, he realized that this slave was unusually intelligent and there was a majesty about him that exceeded any capacity he had seen in his other slaves.

Tom told Settle that he was a proud man and he would rather die than be put to common labor in Settle's fields. The judge was not a gullible man but turned by the slave's tale, he decided to give Tom certain responsibilities on his plantation and before long the slave was functioning credibly as an overseer in the fields.

Tom took a wife and they had children and all were emancipated and found their own way, having taken the Settle name. Tom's son, Reuben and his wife, Mary Brodnax, located on Nubbin Ridge further south in Rockingham County from Judge Settle.

Reuben hired himself to white farmers for a time until he became a share cropper. Such an arrangement gave Reuben inspiration to anticipate the day he could own something of his own. Among the children, he and Mary had a boy that they named Glenn Thomas Settle after his grandfather. Old Tom became the most important influence on the boy's life. He was his teacher and he spent hours telling him about Africa. Nubbin Ridge described an area of red clay that broke through the rich lighter soil around

178

Sandy Cross. It was a small rural black community of share croppers.

In 1902 Reuben Settle, tired of eking out a meager living as a share-cropper and he saw the future of his children as limited. He had enough money to move his family to Uniontown, Pennsylvania where his children were offered a better education.

Glenn Settle's mother repeatedly advised him that, "if white and colored folks got to know each other better, everything would be all right." He developed a strong personal determination as education seemed to liberate him. In 1917 Glenn married Mary Elizabeth Carter and moved with her to Cleveland. He was a janitor, apartment superintendent, truck driver, and warehouseman taking any job in order to get ahead. He was active in the Baptist Church and in 1922 was ordained as a minister.

To expand his education he enrolled in Moody Bible Institute by correspondence. Serving in several churches, he came in 1935 to Gethsemane Baptist Church in Cleveland. He proclaimed at the time, "I have a vision to convince the world that the Negro race is not made up of hoodlums and chicken thieves, but by hard working citizens worthy of this free land."

Music for Glenn was always uplifting to his soul and he loved to sing. Most of his experience with music had been through the church. It was natural that he worked closely with the church choir and became aware of the rising powerful influence of the radio and the rage at the time, the 'hour' programs, mainly religious in their content.

At first, it was simply the housewives,

stenographers, porters, and laborers who gathered regularly at the church to sing. They were serious because they were dedicated and they soon found a reputation attached to their efforts.

They were invited by other churches and civic organizations to perform and their fame as a choral ensemble spread by word of mouth until they quit their jobs and went on the road. On a very small budget, Settle inaugurated the Negro Spiritual Preservation Movement and established "The Negro Hour" in Cleveland. The show aired locally on WGAR beginning in July 1935.

"Wings Over Jordan"-early TV

On January 9, 1938, it debuted nationally over CBS as the "Wings Over Jordan Choir." It was the first full professional black choir in America and the first independently produced national and international radio program created by African Americans.

Korea 1954-Wings Over Jordan-Settle 4th from right

At its height of popularity, the choir performed before sold out audiences in over 45 states, 5 European countries, Canada and Mexico. The radio program was picked up by the BBC and broadcast in England and rebroadcast over Europe.

Under the sponsorship of the USO during World War II, they toured Army camps in Europe. In Viareggio, Italy, for the first time in history, an entire division of the US Army was commanded to attend a choir that performed spiritual music. Afterwards, planes, tanks, and artillery, as well as the men of the 92nd Division, paraded before the reviewing stand as Major General E. M. Almond conferred on the choir the highest citation that civilians can receive from the army. Wings Over Jordan was the only religious

181

group to go overseas during the war. For many Europeans, familiar only with jazz as an American musical art form, Wings Over Jordan was their first experience with Negro Spirituals.

Their fame expanded with the publication of a song book, over 50 recordings, a movie contract, performances with major symphonies, and an invitation to sing at the White House. The choir received the Peabody Award and became the universal voice of American Negroes.

Each year Glenn Settle brought Wings Over Jordan back to perform in Reidsville, his hometown, for his relatives and his former neighbors. Not then allowed into white only hotels and motels, the choir members were housed with individual families.

Seventy-five years later Rockingham County dedicated a North Carolina State Highway Marker to Glenn Settle and Wings Over Jordon. It was the first marker in the county for an African American.

The late June sunset cast a tempered glow along Highway 65 east of Wentworth. The Sheriff and his deputies controlled the normal traffic and passing drivers craned to see what was attracting the crowd. The Velcro-anchored cover was pulled away to reveal the silver and grey marker. Glenn Settle's cousin, Florence Richardson, reminded former Commisioner Harold Bass, "On Sunday mornings I can remember as we walked up the street to church in the summer, we could follow the airing of Wings Over Jordan from house to house."

"Uh huh," responded Bass, remembering the same experience in his Maryland childhood.

182

TEACHING
SUPPLEMENT

The other books of the "Understanding the Flow of Ancestry" series have been set up as narrative events about a common set of slaves as they progressed in individual studies through different locations, functions and changing time. At the end of each study there have been questions designed to lead the students to a more sensitive and interactive discussion of the subject of the particular study.

This volume of the series, deals with branches and generations of the Settle family who lived on a part of the Sauratown Plantation in the 19th century. Like the Farley slaves, the Settle family, in all its various configurations, became a unique context to examine the last half century of slavery in the southern United States. This context extended into the first half century of the national experience in seeking to negotiate those years as they were stigmatized by the static influence of legalized enslavement, justice defined in law and administrated as an instrument of societal segregation, and into an era of contrived denial of justice or civil rights.

This supplement offers each of the chapters of the story of the Settle family for interpretation as historical reality within stifling circumstances. It examines how this one family navigated the ever changing reality of their time with a common, fallible respect for the sanctity of justice as a human right.

Prelude-Highway Marker J-114

The ceremony focusing on the unveiling of a Highway Marker seemed somehow to punctuate this theme. Perhaps it was just a milepost along the way but it was at least distant enough that it seemed to offer a vista for interpretation. When Mrs. Richardson stood before the gathering at the Museum of Rockingham County and said, "I never thought I'd live to see this day," she struck a chord of recognition in everyone present. Standing in that beautiful beige dress, she was the thousand words captured by a picture.

The Douglas Inheritance

In the antebellum period of American history, enslavement and abolition were the extremes of the issue that allowed ownership of one person by another. The system of slavery had evolved within the events of the growth of the country. The debate had its separate platforms in religion, politics, and economics. It was in the latter that slavery became a metastasized cancer.

Stephen A. Douglas was able to build a political career debating a balancing of slavery within the law. He could portray himself as the reasonable adult able to navigate through nuance and prejudice toward an acceptable compromise. What he was doing in the 1850s was exactly what the founding fathers were doing in 1787, taking an issue structured in the law and making it tolerable within the practice. This issue was bound in human ethics

185

as a contradiction of justice. It was not possible to forever espouse human dignity and simultaneously legalize against it.

Like others before him, Douglas could build his career on compromise in a democratic form but as the historian, Hendrik Van Loon said, there is a point at which someone says, "closing time gentlemen."

Douglas surely saw that conundrum when he met the cousin of his seatmate in Congress, Martha Martin of Rockingham County, North Carolina. Representative David Settle Reid said, "she is a beautiful daughter and she is so rich." Douglas' discovery, after already being wounded by cupid's arrow, was that a major portion of her wealth was constituted in slaves in North Carolina and Mississippi.

When his future father-in-law, at the point of the engagement, attempted to give him a Mississippi Plantation, Douglas had to plead against his own good fortune. "Please, sir, I cannot return to Illinois and claim impartiality when I myself own slaves. You cannot make me such a gift."

The solution that they worked out mirrored all the compromise and accommodations of law and society made in the face of personal hypocrisy. All the wealth would pass to Martha Martin Douglas and through to her heirs, and Douglas would manage the estate and be paid accordingly. He could claim, as he was forced to do many times in the course of his subsequent Presidential Campaign against Lincoln in 1860, that he "owned no slaves." By 1860 it was too late for Douglas' compromises.

By then Douglas had already brought the body of his beautiful Martha home to be buried in North Carolina and he was managing the plantations for his two small sons. Douglas lived only three months after Lincoln was inaugurated but the details of the ownership of some of that land were still being litigated in the courts of Mississippi in 1877, the year Reconstruction ended with the withdrawal of Federal Troops from the South.

Washington, a Slave

The story of the young slave, Washington, demonstrates the pathos in any age, at the death of a youth. In this case that smarting of grief can surface during a river cleanup as well as in the instant of a hunting accident. The boy is half white and half black but he is universal in terms of the emotional reaction that he engenders.

Washington seems to give context to the story of Josiah and Nancy Ann Settle, his parents. He merges all the variables of a race based society and funnels them into the futile loss of a child. The rest of the story seems only to be background.

My Intended Wife and Children

The marriage of Josiah Settle and Frances Graves is a too familiar repetition of the merger of two patriarchal plantation families. Giving variance to this particular wedding was the fact that two sisters were now married to two brothers. Thomas and Josiah Settle married Henrietta and Frances Graves and Thomas' twin sister had married

Robert Martin and was the mother of Martha Martin Douglas.

As a gift of her parents, Frances brought to her marriage a slave girl, Nancy Ann, who was a mulatto. This meant she was the daughter of a white man and was a slave because the child of a slave woman was by law a slave. Any male in the Graves family would be a prime suspect as the father of Nancy Ann but some descendents of this family make the claim that Azariah Graves, father of Henrietta and Frances was also the father of Nancy Ann. Jane Austin redux.

Frances Settle died while giving birth to her second daughter in 1829. Josiah was left with the care of the two young daughters and probably it was to Nancy Ann that the family turned in order for her to act as the nurse. Nancy Ann bore Washington a year later.

Within the family circle, the relationship between Nancy Ann and Josiah was at least discomforting. It was not a unique situation within the plantation society and the slaves in the quarters were certainly fully aware of the circumstances. In the main house, the existence of a child of mixed parentage was commonly masked or veiled from sight as long as possible.

When Nancy Ann then continued to have another child by Josiah every two years, the relationship became part of the dynamics in the Settle family. Thomas and Henrietta's children, the daughters of Mary Martin, and Josiah's two daughters, all contemporaries, played together and became schoolmates. The inter-personal relationships

188

were familial, but the posture of the children and the adults were each tinged with the racial contradiction of the time.

For Josiah and Nancy, the remaining record seems to present a kind of marital ambivalence not brought on by a sexual indifference but by the distortion of racial bias. A clue to the practice of this unnatural bias may be the system of naming that was adopted, obviously by Josiah. Instead of incorporating for his mulatto children, any of the family names popular with the Settles, he named his first six sons for political leaders in spite of the fact that he was not a politician.

This story cannot be told without the acknowledgement that major characters: Azariah Graves, Tyre Glenn, and Josiah Settle, were all at one time or another, successful slave traders. This seems to be a contradictory influence on the flow of the narrative. All the generational commitment: the opposition to the practice of slavery, to the end of slavery in the South, and to reconstruction of a fractured nation based on equitable treatment of the former slaves, is hard to see as coming out of the family connections with the slave trade.

Whatever attracted Josiah to Nancy Ann, whether it was proximity or beauty, she was the product of a system that denied her education, social exposure, or religious training. She spoke the language of the quarters although she had some exposure to life in the big house. Could she ever be comfortable in a situation of which she had never expected to be a part? The review of their life together is always a study of dichotomy in flux.

189

The death of Washington was a catalytic moment, something that thrusts all the social concerns to the shadows. At that moment, Nancy Ann was not mulatto or half-sister or concubine. She was a mother in grief. Nothing else mattered to her. She could for the first time, surrender to a visceral center dependent on no other time, place, circumstance, or person. As Nancy Ann recovered from the intense shock, she had been reconstituted. From that point forward, while it was Josiah who made decisions about location, it was Nancy Ann who progressively maneuvered the relationship she intended for her family.

The plantation in Mississippi was Josiah's choice, a wise investment in an agricultural economy with which he had been involved all his life. It almost promised to be a financial success. For Nancy Ann, it was the way to cut all the tentacles of race and rejection that she recognized had strangled her relationship with Josiah. If Josiah had any reservations about moving from North Carolina to Mississippi, Nancy Ann's enthusiasm for the change was a motivating force. She was able to use his decision based solely on economics, to satisfy her determination to get away from the stifling presence of the family.

Mississippi was another matter. Josiah already had slaves there and he brought more from North Carolina. Nancy Ann and her children, by applicable definition, were part of his slave community. In Mississippi, however, she could move into the big house. She could subsume the function of "mistress of the mansion." She was enabled to make choices. Her children were the master's children. Every attempt she made to establish herself in this role was anathema to the rest of the slave community. She had replaced the stifling standards of the Settles for the jealousy of the quarters.

Nancy Ann began to pressure Josiah to recognize that, with her mulatto children, they were a family. Her children should not be raised as slaves. He had to manumit them and their mother. The laws of North Carolina and Mississippi were the same on one point at least. A slave once freed by a master had to leave the state within the year. If it had been Josiah who sought to free his family, he could have done it at the point that they left North Carolina and then they would have been free blacks coming into Mississippi. Then Nancy Ann would have lacked another justification for leaving Mississippi and the South altogether. It may be too much to credit Nancy with such calculation but now freeing her family was the motivation to move out of the slave states.

Butler County, Ohio was immediately north of Cincinnati and the Ohio River. It was possible to go down the Ohio to Paducah, Kentucky and pick up the Tennessee River to Tishomingo County, Mississippi or use the Mississippi River. So Josiah had easy access to his plantation and moving his family did not take away his investment potential. It was clear that by moving his family to Ohio, Josiah was willing to place some distance on relationships and that Nancy Ann was agreeable to the arrangement.

Leaving Paducah on the way north meant leaving the slave states and Ohio was a non-slave state. Thus the mixed family, freed legally, was free from the debilitating

191

laws of slavery. Perhaps more immediately important, it meant that the children would have access to a level of education not available in North Carolina or Mississippi.

Josiah bought his family a house and this time Nancy Ann could truly take on the role of mistress. The slaves were in Mississippi. She became a housewife with a large family. Although there were few free blacks in Hanover Township, the neighbors were welcoming. Then somehow word got out that Josiah and Nancy were not married. Race did not become an issue but propriety did. Partly as an effort to appease and partly to satisfy Nancy's growing determination to be the mistress of her family of children, Josiah bought and moved into a separate house next door. Society would not be appeased, so a marriage was planned with all the children present. The children saw it as a celebration not recognizing that by law they were now considered legitimate.

Josiah sold his plantation in Mississippi in 1859 not to please Nancy. He was a Unionist. This was important because here he was in harmony with others in his family. Most of his actions after the death of his first wife abrogated the institution of slavery. The exception was significant. He owned slaves and brought more to the Mississippi plantation. He was characteristic of the southern plantation owner who was the sinner who hated the sin - infamous in the face of nobility. The sale of the plantation was fortuitous and probably calculated. He saw the coming conflict as the end of the institution and thus surely financial ruin. He sold his land and slaves before emancipation wiped out half the value of his property.

Navigating the story of Josiah and Nancy Ann requires a pragmatic appreciation of the conundrums of slavery.

Thomas Settle, Unionist

The narrative of Thomas Settle, Jr., builds on that of his uncle, Josiah. Thomas was the triumphant success of his parents. There was no satisfaction greater than a politician and superior court judge whose son became a gubernatorial candidate and Justice of the State Supreme Court. It was almost scripted success.

Thomas Settle was a Whig. Through his first position, after graduating from the University, he was private secretary for his cousin Democratic Governor David Settle Reid. Thomas Settle, Jr. became a Democrat. His first cousin had married Democratic Senator Stephen A. Douglas. All these men were staunch Unionists.

After young Thomas finished reading law under Richmond Pearson, he entered into practice in Rockingham County and the surrounding judicial district. He was almost immediately elected to the North Carolina House of Commons and four years later was chosen Speaker of the Commons. He married Mary Glenn of Yadkin County whom he probably met while a student at Pearson's law school. Her father was Tyre Glenn, a slave trader, whiskey maker, iron monger, merchant, very large plantation owner, and fierce Unionist.

Thomas Settle and David Settle Reid were among the leaders in North Carolina in opposition to secession from the Union at the time of the state convention.

Senator Douglas as a politician and Presidential candidate, avidly supported the preservation of the Union through every effort at compromise.

Thomas got blind-sided by Lincoln's call to North Carolina for troops to fight against the Confederate States. In his rush to preserve his political viability, he proclaimed his former position as error and rushed to enlist. After a year of service as a Captain of a Company of Rockingham County troops, he recognized he was unable to fight and to lead young men to die for a cause to which he was opposed. It could have been his darkest hour and indeed it was a cloud that hung over the rest of his political life. Had his story ended at this point, history would surely have seen him as disingenuous at least and a coward at best. Everything that followed in his life demonstrated his commitment to the cause of the Union, reconstruction of the nation, and Black suffrage, even at the risk of rejection and assassination.

I believe that Thomas Settle's Spring Garden Speech on June 22, 1867, was the finest recitation of a just and practical course of Reconstruction and was a worthy extension of Abraham Lincoln's intentions in his Second Inaugural Speech two years before.

Tyre Glenn thwarted a plot designed to lure him from his Glenwood plantation and hang him as a Unionist traitor. His brother in Tennessee was hung by Confederate vigilantes as a Union sympathizer. At least three planned assassination attempts against Thomas Settle, one in the yard of his home, convinced him that his family was at risk and he moved them to Greensboro. Even David Settle Reid,

194

a former Governor, felt so threatened that he moved from his Dan River plantation across from Settle, to Wentworth.

The Klan was more virulent in Caswell County but they also burned and murdered in Rockingham. It took men of deep conviction to pursue a career aspiring to higher office in the state. Otherwise, it was men who saw prejudice against the free slaves as a route to office through demagoguery. This contrast of motives should not be extended so far as to indicate saints and sinners. There were plenty of both on each side of the motives.

"The Battle of Giants," the Gubernatorial Campaign in North Carolina between wartime Governor Zebulon B. Vance and Thomas Settle, Jr., encapsulated the Reconstruction era in the state. Vance's election would be a return to the past, to the rancor of Secession, and it would set the character of the Democratic Party in North Carolina for almost a century. Settle saw, and projected for the electorate, that he and the Republican Party intended to find a path from outlawed slavery, to a period of racial justice. He visualized that only through racial harmony could the state build viability in the industrial age. Pitting the races at a time of minimal industrial wages, may have been an avenue to electoral success but it restricted the potential of profit to the upper class. Vance's victory sealed the issue.

Impeachment

Robert Martin Douglas lost his mother when he was three and his famous father when he was only twelve. His grandmother, Mary Settle Martin had died the year before

195

at her plantation in Rockingham County which had been his second home after his mother's early death. His teen years were under the care of his stepmother, Adele Cutts, and she remarried in 1866 when he was seventeen.

He and his brother, Steven were heirs of all the extensive interests of their mother in North Carolina and Mississippi but Robert was provided his grandparent's 900 acre plantation. By making this specific bequest, Mary Martin had left a strong reason for Robert to settle in North Carolina in spite of the choices that he obviously had, in Illinois, Washington, or Mississippi.

Robert found the immediate position as Private Secretary to Governor Holden obviously because of who he was. Then within a year he had gone to work in the same position for the President of the United States. He knew that such success had not come entirely on his own merit.

Kirk's War and the appearance of the Ku Klux Klan in Piedmont North Carolina was heavily concentrated in the midst of the neighborhood that Douglas intended to make his home. In Raleigh and in Washington, he was the available resource for analysis of the background events that had brought the violence of the post Civil War onto a level that could be characterized as a 'war.' He was the resource who knew the people and the location.

Douglas was also in place when Grant succeeded in the passage of the second of the amendments to the Constitution concerning the legal ending of slavery and its structure, the 15th Amendment. This amendment concerned suffrage and it is significant that Douglas' career seems to have been spent defending Negro suffrage. When the

Democratic Party succeeded in the "redemption" of white supremacy in North Carolina at the end of the century, it was at the expense of Negro suffrage.

With his Negro cousin, Josiah Settle, Douglas was in Washington, and both were in a focal position at a critical moment. In their personal experiences, they embodied the essence of the repositioning struggle we refer to as Reconstruction, which was in process. Their conversation would have allowed this second generation to make an evaluation of the slavery experience within their own family. They would have known that their circumstances were somewhat more complicated than in most families. Such discussions did take place as, within the family unit, the events surrounding the Civil War and Emancipation, were processed.

The Freedmen's Bureau was the Washington bureaucratic structure that sought to navigate the former slaves into freedom. It was born to inevitably be a flashpoint in the face of victory and defeat. Combined with the withdrawal of Federal troops from the South, the end of the Freedmen's Bureau defined the end of the Reconstruction experience in America. Josiah was in many ways, a success of the Bureau. He was able to graduate and get his Law Degree through Howard University, which was itself a direct byproduct of the Bureau's efforts. He worked for a time within the Bureau and by choosing to return to Mississippi to practice law, he personified the best aim and purpose of that institution.

The recognition of the differing influence of slaves as an ethnic group and slaves defined by race, is a more recent academic debate. It is appropriate, however, to hear it discussed in this contemporary setting between Bob and Joe.

The successful impeachment of Governor William Holden has particular impact as it preceded the unsuccessful attempt to impeach Douglas. Holden's actions in light of the insurrection in Caswell and Rockingham, had obviously averted an even greater insurrection that might have spread widely. The degree of his specific actions under the state constitution, was a very partisan debate.

Douglas, for a second time, returned to North Carolina and this time he succeeded in making it his home. He passed over a location at the Martin Plantation choosing instead the more commercial town of Greensboro. He found his wife through his connection with the legal profession. Judge Robert P. Dick had actually begun his successful legal career in Wentworth just a few years before Robert had been born. He thus was acquainted with Douglas' family.

The period of Fusion Party politics in North Carolina reads like a drama. The old residual battles of Unionists versus Secessionists, of slavery and enfranchisement, dressed in new causes as Negro suffrage and white supremacy, seemed to be overtaken by a Depression that inspired a farmer's rebellion. The Republicans were the beneficiary because they were the first to fuse with the Populists to claim a majority. Odd bedfellows, it was in this period that Douglas became a member of the state supreme court. The effort of the Democrats, as retribution after regaining the majority, to impeach the Republican justices on the court, was an historical embarrassment. Douglas retained the highest reputation in his profession.

Joe

Josiah Thomas Settle, "Joe," was the youngest grandson of old David and Rhoda Settle, and a slave, of General Azariah Graves, who had been raped by a member of the Graves family. He was a first cousin of the wife of Senator Stephen A. Douglas, whom he probably never met. He was also the first cousin of Thomas Settle, Jr. and of Governor David Settle Reid, through the latter's wife, and nephew of Senator Calvin Graves.

His life can be considered an allegory for the human transition from enslavement in the South to enlightened opportunity in the country in the last half of the 19th century. For most families and individuals, the progression came in the next century. The earlier transition was often as a result of some consanguinity. In Joe's case, his father was white and his mother was a slave. Also, his father's family seemed to be uniformly and aggressively in favor of an end to slavery and all of its debilitating effects.

Joe was conceived in circumstances where he would have by law been a slave. He was born physically while the family was in transition - in route. He was freed from slavery in the heart of the slave-driven Cotton South. He found access to education at the moment he came to school age. He came in contact with a white teacher and she taught him that justice was an inter-personal word. His father was a slave owner dependent on the system for his economic future. His mother was a strong-willed mulatto who found empowerment within herself to rise above a system. All these thing were fortuitous circumstances into which Joe was born.

Out of his own fortitude he found and knew to pursue education. He pioneered among his race the new institutional education being inaugurated in American for Blacks. He drove for excellence. He thrived on exposure to opportunity. At the point of success, he turned back to those who were still unfulfilled. He went not to Washington or Ohio but to Mississippi and Tennessee. He gained offices not previously available to black citizens and performed them admirably. He set the standards others could follow and the skeptical could recognize as possible. Only then, did he turn back and concentrate on the similar needs of his family.

He also felt a responsibility as among the first graduates of Howard University. His correspondence with such people as Frederick Douglas and Oliver Otis Howard, founder and president of Howard, confirm his loyalty to the school and his broad national connection to Negro leadership.

In a time in history, when rampant, pernicious segregation was being perpetrated on the Negro by legislators, elected out of ignorance by fear and prejudice, Joe was able to succeed even in the face of that system that perverted against him.

Nubbin Ridge

Glenn T. Settle knew that his roots were in the slave quarters at the Thomas Settle home place. One of the only roots he had to his African heritage was his love of music of the spirit. His mother was convinced that there was a way, a bridge, by which the white man and the colored man could live in harmony and she intended that her boy would find it.

It was Glenn's father, Reuben, who led his people away toward more promise. It was the immigrant step that has moved the human race. It was not dramatic in every generation. In some it was simply a latent yearning.

Glenn combined the hunger of his parents when he established the Negro Spiritual Preservation Movement and "The Negro Hour" in Cleveland in 1935. He grasped two significant contemporary opportunities. The first was the need to capture the Negro Spiritual as an American art form and to find the means to preserve it. The pentatonic scale which was so often found in these spirituals was his link to the African past. He had no personal wealth to make this possible but he established the mechanism knowing that inspiration would breed opportunity. Second, he saw radio, the first electronic media, as the vehicle of distribution into millions of homes. The "Hour" programs implied relaxing, taking time to enjoy, and they connected people to a familiar core.

Settle, all his professional life, ran into malice and prejudice. Part of his home community welcomed him yearly to enjoy the gift of music that he brought to them, but the rest of that community would not let him partake of any public services because he was a black man. He was still aware that in the human condition, malice and prejudice can be tolerated at perhaps 3 parts per 100 - human frailty. When that percentage begins to go higher, we are faced with a cancer upon the public dignity.

It is through Glenn that this story connected with the Second World War when America was socially transformed - not purified. He took a particular musical form that originated once in Africa and introduced it to a public of young men and women who were certain they were defending human rights. The enjoyment of that music was an inter-personal experience. Walking up the street on Sunday morning and hearing the unifying power of the Negro Spiritual pass from home to home, every African American began to feel verified. Watching a black choir perform music on a stage touched their soul and made every soldier feel verified.

Glenn Settle's Wings Over Jordan music helped measurably in setting the themes for the dreams of a Martin Luther King in the second half of the century.

EDITOR'S NOTES

This manuscript is the product of many years of research. In order to expand the content to a more teachable text, I have added to it my own interpretive dialogue. I have also taken an author's license to interpret some situations and to make some conclusions about circumstances that are not "in evidence." In a courtroom world these might be considered "out of order" or "not proven."

In this "Editor's Notes" section, I am going to clarify my sources in more detail and flag, for a researcher, the extent of the recorded data from which it was made. This will give a better basis for debate and should encourage further research toward a more scholarly conclusion.

"The Settle Family Journey Through Slavery" covers a period of time from about 1840 through 2013. It has a common company of characters in the Settle family, black and white. It has a common theme of the individual struggle within a single family, to cope with slavery, a moral contradiction, and the diverse attempts to reconstruct the relationship of community when, following the Civil War, the goal became justice. The Settle family and their close associates, are represented in this struggle because there seems to be such a strong commitment to justice built upon the themes of the Constitution of the United States. While many of their white neighbors used the bitterness of defeat, the fear of class and race, and the suspicion of ignorance, to demagogue their way to political dominance, this family exhibited a strong adherence to the Union of the states and commitment to the opportunities that would come from racial harmony within an expanding economy.

The racial diversity within the family made certain that even the commonly held respect for racial justice, came with nuance and self oriented perspective. Good will and blood relationship did not guarantee acceptance but it did encourage respect in debate. Sometimes that can be the beginning of reconciliation.

Highway Marker J-114

The events surrounding the erection of the North Carolina Highway Marker to Glenn T. Settle, are all true and became an inspiration that seemed to bring the diverse subjects of the book together. Names of some contemporary people have been changed.

The Douglas Inheritance

Martha Martin Douglas, wife of Senator Stephen A. Douglas of Illinois, died in Washington January 19, 1853 a day after her un-named daughter was born. The daughter died after about a week. Martha's funeral was at her Washington home at noon on Saturday, January 22nd.. Her body and probably that of her baby were brought home to Rockingham County by her husband and mother, to be buried beside her father and sister. They had to make stops along the way and such a stop is imagined at Bachelor's Hall which might have been an appropriate distance for the final leg of the journey. I have assumed the presence of

Martha's children accompanying their parents. Mary Martin was on the trip and I have created the discussions with Douglas related to the future of the boys, none of which were recorded.

All the political circumstances regarding Douglas are true and come from accepted authority. I have tried to interpret his thoughts from a close reading of existing letters and texts. This is not, however, a biography of Douglas. It only attempts to capture what might have been his influence on the subject of the book and upon his southern in-laws.

The Settle Cemetery is a pivotal and real location in Rockingham County and the several descriptions of the layout of the cemetery are correct. The conclusion that Governor Alexander Martin, Jane Hunter Martin, and Robert Martin were moved from the family crypt and buried at the Settle Cemetery, is mine based on many years of research. It is known that they were moved. Robert Martin Douglas, in a speech many years later at Guilford Courthouse Battlefield, mentioned the removal but said that the place of burial was unknown. That was strange under the circumstances.

The Thomas Settle House is real but I have assumed it as the location for the assembly after the funeral. I have tried to place people at that wake who I think might have been there. There is no extant list of attendees.

Thomas Settle, Junior, was in the process of taking over ownership of the Alfred M. Scales house at Mulberry Island. Thomas Settle, Junior had just been at Judge Richmond Pearson's Law School.

This is the first of several times that I refer to Azariah Graves as the father of both Josiah Settle's first wife and his slave wife. There are claims in genealogies of the descendents of Nancy Ann Grave Settle, that she was Azariah's daughter and therefore half-sister of Frances Graves Settle and Henrietta Graves Settle. I think it is clear from her identification in the Census that she was a mulatto and by the surviving photograph of Nancy Ann, that she had white blood. I would feel almost certain to say that she was fathered by someone in the Azariah Graves family. It may not have been Azariah himself although I have used that assumption.

The children do appear to have been left with their grandmother, Mary Martin, at this time. The Martin plantations are as described.

Stephen Douglas did lapse into alcohol in this period of grief and his friends feared for his life. The trip to Europe was an attempt to dry out and rebuild his life.

Mary Martin's excursion to the Settle Cemetery with the boys is imagination although it was surely made at some time and Mary had many opportunities to assist the children in processing their grief.

The problems that Douglas experienced, at the time of his betrothal to Martha Deneen Martin as to her inheritance, is true. It is an example of how slavery could cast a pall over the simplest of circumstances and the lingering issues that surrounded the end of that institution. Robert Martin did make the residual arrangements to have his slaves sent back and financed in Africa should there be no direct heirs

The collusion indicated between Mary Martin and the Grangers (Douglas' sister and husband) in Washington is clear from letters. The introduction of a step-mother in Adele Cutts, was rocky and seems not to have been helped by the maneuvers of Mary and the Grangers behind the backs of the newlyweds. Adele was to have a great deal of influence over Robert and Stevie, particularly after Mary Martin and Stephen Douglas died.

The discussion of the 1872 Court Case in Mississippi, is authentic.

Washington, a Slave

The experience with the theft and return of the tombstone for Washington, is all true.

My Intended Wife and Children

The background about the Settles and Graves families is from records or manuscripts. The reaction to the knowledge that Josiah Settle had a child and then children by Nancy Ann, a slave, is based on circumstance as I interpret them. Some form of these discussions must have taken place and they reflect the circumstances and persons who would have been involved.

Josiah was a well known slave trader. It had been that business that had given him familiarity with the Cotton South. The contradiction always existed, once a slave trader, was it possible to ever have a sincere emotion for a slave? Especially while by a slave, you were producing more slaves?

The nature of the relationship, bordered on scandal in spite of the fact that white masters having children by their slaves, was so very common. There might have been even more scandal except that most people were afraid to throw the first stone. This story is a good study of the levels and types of concealment woven through each family - like a weft that appears through the warp on the loom distinguishing the design.

Thomas Settle had particular reason to react strongly to Josiah's children by Nancy Ann. His wife and Josiah's wife, Frances, were sisters. Whatever blood relationship Nancy Ann had through the Graves family to them was an embarrassment. Again the debate between the brothers and with Josiah's parents, is my imagination but similar conversations certainly occurred under the circumstances.

The discussions between Josiah and Nancy Ann are all my creations. In these discussions, the social separation between master and slave had been breached but not by equals. Intimacy was strained. The knowledge of the relationship between master and slave had a similar reaction within the slave community. Time regularly shuffled these relationships and they had to be re-aligned over the years. This put a repeated strain on any inter-personal relationship.

The census records report Nancy and her children as slaves. I am presuming that Josiah and Nancy lived apart in North Carolina but in Mississippi they could have lived as a family. The records in Ohio and family descriptions, say they lived apart.

Elizabeth and Frances lived as Josiah's children in the David Settle home under the care of their widowed grandmother.

The brick schoolhouse at the Judge Thomas Settle home did exist until it was removed for a highway widening about 1963. The assumption that girls and at least some of Nancy's children attended, is not documented.

The various moves from North Carolina to the Cotton South by sons of plantation owners is true and those mentioned are accurate. This shift from the experience of a tobacco economy to a cotton based agricultural economy did play a determinative part in the movement of people in the South including the slaves. There were more tobacco factories in Rockingham County than in any other county in North Carolina and Mississippi probably drew more of the plantation owners from North Carolina.

I have taken license in recording the story of the Christmas Day accident in which Washington was killed. The only record is from the tombstone. The sequence of the moves made by Josiah and Nancy are accurate. I superimposed facts about time, place, politics, and events in order to re-construct what might have been the motives and stimulants behind these moves. The records of the descendants of Josiah and Nancy provided some clues.

At the time Josiah and Nancy left North Carolina, Elizabeth and Frances Settle were courting and marrying men of good family from Caswell County. They did not need to go with their father and the fact that they would be

210

settled with new husbands, probably helped precipitate the timing of their father's move. Both daughters and husbands settled in Georgia. *No.*

One unanswered question is why, since both states had laws that freed slaves had to leave the state within a year of having gained their freedom, did Josiah not simply free Nancy and the children in North Carolina. Then they would have been free when they got to Mississippi and would not be bound to leave there when he did manumit them. I dealt with this issue based on unsupported conclusions.

The names that were chosen for the sons of Josiah and Nancy have such a clear pattern and they do avoid the use of Settle family first names. The relationship of the naming practice to the Settle family circumstances is my interpretation.

The appearance of conflict between Nancy and her children on one side and the rest of the slaves on the other has been re-created. There were always subtle frictions, within which slavery functioned, that went beyond the obvious ones between master and slave. There were few rewards for the slave so any appearance of favoritism was likely to produce anything from suspicion to violence.

The trip to Ohio was also manufactured but something of the kind certainly preceded the move of the family from Mississippi. Josiah did manumit his family before they left Mississippi. When they went north, they were free blacks so would have had little difficulty crossing out of the slave states. They did not need to be part of the Underground Railroad.

The story of the reaction in Butler County, to the fact that they were not married, comes from family history as does the fact that they did not live together but in two houses next to each other. *also census*

Thomas Settle, Unionist

The events of April 14, 1861 come from a record written by Judge Howard. The words of Settle's speech in Madison are my creation based on Howard's record. Mulberry Island did exist but I have created the dialogue of the men at Mulberry Island debating the oncoming of the war and their intentions about how to deal with it.

The events on Court Day in Wentworth are true. The events surrounding Thomas Settle's resignation are all accurate. The dialogue was written around the events to give context. The relationship with Chalmers Glenn is accurate.

The wake at Sauratown, following receipt of the news of Chalmers Glenn's death, is my creation although something very like that must have happened. The comments about the thoughts that Enoch had from what he heard that day are my creation. They recognize the layers of communication through which information was passed on the plantation. They also show that the slaves had to process information for themselves. They were not part of the conversation and they were not given "white papers" or bulletins.

The incident in 1864 in Wentworth during the Vance - Holden Campaign comes from eyewitnesses and the accuracy was verified by Settle himself.

The excerpts from the Spring Garden Speech on June 22 1867 are also quoted verbatim although some of the setting is my construction. The experiences related to the Ku Klux Klan are from facts reported at the time. The Vance - Settle Campaign is all fact.

Impeachment

The information about the young Robert Martin Douglas is factual as is the family generational chart. He was appointed private secretary to Governor William W. Holden and an initial conversation must have happened although I have imagined the content. All the report of the Ku Klux Klan activity is as it was reported at the time. I have taken some liberties in pointing out the obvious contributions of Douglas, because of who he was and who he knew, in the co-operative attitude of the Grant administration with Holden's action in the state. Bob and Joe were in a particularly unique position in the time because of their family connections.

The young men were in Washington at this moment in history. They certainly knew of each other through the family but probably never had met. All their circumstances converged in such a way that they must have met there and established a relationship of like interests. Because one was considered black and one white, they had an intersection in time that was extraordinary.

The impeachment of Governor Holden is true but again I have developed the interaction of Bob and Joe out of the actual circumstances. In Bob, this impeachment is prophetic in anticipating his own. There is a synergistic atmosphere to these relationships.

Bob's return to Greensboro, his marriage and his success in passing the bar are all facts. The discussion of North Carolina Politics at the end of the 19th century is true and it seems to be a validation of Douglas' political will and vindication of the commitment that he and Josiah Thomas Settle had reached in their Washington discussions as young men.

The recital of Douglas' experience as a justice of the state supreme court is factual but here its particular importance is in demonstrating that some of his political success was based on the application of patronage. At the same time it shows that his opponents were willing to resort to violence, pretext, spurious claims, disenfranchisement, lies, murder, and open rejection of the proclamation of democracy, in order to suppress the former slaves. Much of this information was reviewed with centenarian Dick Douglas, Robert M. Douglas' grandson and is covered thoroughly by him in "Impeaching North Carolina Supreme Court Justices a Hundred Years Ago" in the North Carolina State Bar Journal. Additional direction came from conversations with Danny Moody, historian, for the North Carolina Supreme Court.

Joe

The conversation between Joe and Josiah has been manufactured to set up Joe's story. It probably took place over a period of time in bits and pieces. Joe's experience with the white female teacher comes from his biography.

The record of his education at Oberlin and Howard is accurate. He was among the first former slaves to benefit so directly from the work of the Freedman's Bureau and he was consequently very motivated.

The conversation between Thomas Settle, Jr. and Josiah T. Settle at the Republican National Convention in 1876, is my construction. Both were present and it seems likely that it took place in some form.

The record of Joe's political career comes from his biography. The quotation from the St. Louis Globe Democrat and Joe's quotation at the end of his active political career are accurate.

Nubbin Ridge

The conversation between Judge Thomas Settle and the slave, Tom, is reported in Glenn Settle's biography to have happened but I have made up the dialogue. The biography asserts the claim that Tom was a King.

The record of Glenn T. Settle's life comes from various public biographies.

The dedication of the Highway Marker was as described and comes from my conversation on that day with Mrs. Florence Richardson and Harold Bass.

BIBLIOGRAPHY

MANUSCRIPT COLLECTIONS -COURT RECORDS - CENSUS RECORDS. - LETTERS

Ancestry.com - Census Records
>MS Toshomingo Co - 1860, 1870
>OH Butler Co. 1860, 1870, 1875 (Map), 1880
>NC Rockingham Co. 1820, 1830, 1840,1850, 1860, 1870, 1880
>NC Caswell Co. 1820, 1830

Dick Douglas to author: November 19, 2013

Francie Lane to author: 1/11/99, 2/10/99, 5/4/10 all concerning Drennen family association with Robert Martin

Henry County Court Minutes, Bassett, VA.

Howard University Manuscript Collection (www.howard.edu
>Josiah Thomas Settle

Rockingham County, NC Court Minutes

Rockingham County, Deed Books

Rockingham County, NC Wills and Estate Records.

Stephan A. Douglas Papers, University of Chicago

BOOKS AND PUBLIC RECORDS

- Anderson, Eric, **Race and Politics in North Carolina 1872-1901**, Baton Rouge: Louisana State University Press, 1981
- Bassett, John Spencer, **Anti-Slavery Leaders of North Carolina**, Baltimore: The Johns Hopkins Press, 1898

Battle, Kemp P. **History of the University of North Carolina**, I Raleigh: Edwards & Broughton Press, 1907

_____, **Biographical Directory of the American Congress, 1771-1961**, Washington: Government Printing Office, 1961

      David Settle Reid,
      Stephen A. Douglas
      Thomas Settle

Bisher, Catherine W., Charlotte V. Brown, Carla R. Lounsbury, Ernest H. Wood, III. **Architects and Builders in North Carolina, A History of the Practice of Building**, Chapel Hill: The University of North Carolina Press, 1990

Bolton, Charles C. **Poor Whites of the Antebellum South, Tenants and Laborers in Central North Carolina and Northern Mississippi**, Durham: Duke University Press, 1994

Brown, Claudia Robert. **A Tale of Three Cities, Eden Heritage: A Pictorial Survey of Leaksville, Spray & Draper**. Historic Properties Commission, 1996

Butler, Lindley S. **Our Proud Heritage - A Pictorial History of Rockingham County, NC**. Bassett: The Bassett Publishing Company, 1971.

Butler, Lindley S., **The Papers of David Settle Reid 1829-1852**, I, Chapel Hill: The University of North Carolina Press, 1993

Butler, Lindley S., **The Papers of David Settle Reid, 1853-1913**, II, Chapel Hill: The University of North Carolina Press, 1997

Capers, Gerald M. **Stephen A. Douglas, Defender of the Union**, Boston: Little, Brown and Company, 1959

Censers, Jane Turner, **North Carolina Planters and Their Children**, Baton Rouge: Louisiana State University Press, 1984.

Crow, Jeffrey J., & Flora J. Hatley, edited, **Black Americans in North Carolina and the South**, Chapel Hill:The University of North Carolina Press, 1984.

Crow, Jeffrey J. **The Black Experience in Revolutionary North Carolina**. Raleigh: Division of Archives and History, 1977.

Dibble, Roy F.,**Albion W. Tourgée**, Washington, NY, Kennikat Press, 1968 reprint

DeCosta-Willis, Miriam, **Notable Black Memphians**, Google Books

Egerton, Douglas R. 02 **Gabriel's Rebellion, The Virginia Slave Conspiracies of 1800 & 1802,** Chapel Hill: University of North Carolina Press, 1993.
Federal Census 1820 to 1910 inclusive 1860.Rockingham County, NC.

Foote, Rev. William Henry, **Sketches of North Carolina Historical and Biographical,** New York: Robert Carter, 1846

Foner, Eric, **Reconstruction, America's Unfinished Revolution, 1863-1877**, New York, History Book Club, 1988

Gross, Theodore L., Albion W. Tourgée, New York: Twayne Publishers, 1963

Hairston, Peter W. **The Cooleemee Plantation and Its People**. Winston Salem: Hunter Publishing, 1986.

Hamilton, J. G. De Roulac. **Papers of Thomas Ruffin**, Vol. I. Raleigh: Edwards & Broughton, 1915

Harris, William C. **William Woods Holden, Firebrand of North Carolina Politics**, Baton Rouge: Louisiana State University Press, 1987

Johannsen, Robert W., **Stephen A. Douglas**, New York, Oxford University Press, 1975.

Johannsen, Robert W., editor, **The Letters of Stephen A. Douglas**, Urbana: University of Illinois Press, 1961

Johanson, Allen, **Stephen A. Douglas, A Study in American Ploitics**, New York: The Macmillan Company, 1908

Johnson, Guion Griffin. **Anti-Bellum North Carolina, A Social History,** Chapel Hill: The University of North Carolina Press, 1937.

Jordan, Weymount T., Jr., **North Carolina Troops 1861-1865 A Roster**,V, Raleigh: Division of Archives and History, 1975.

Koncle, Henry G., **John Motley Morehead and the Development of North Carolina 1796-1866**, Philadelphia: William J. Campbell, 1922

Lefler, Hugh Talmage & Albert Ray Newsome, **The History of a Southern State, North Carolina**, Chapel Hill: The University of North Carolina Press, 1954

O'Brien, Gail Williams, **The Legal Fraternity and the Making of a New Southern Community 1848-188**2, Athens: University Press of Georgia, 1986.

- Powell, William S., **North Carolina, Through Four Centuries**, Chapel Hill: The University of North Carolina Press, 1989
- Powell, William S., **Dictionary of North Carolina Biography**, Vol. 6 & 7, Chapel Hill: University of North Carolina Press, 1996.
- Raper, Horace W., **William W. Holden: North Carolina Political Enigma**, Chapel Hill: University of North Carolina Press, 1985.
- Reid, Paul Apperson, **Gubernatorial Campaigns and Administrations of David S. Reid, 1848-1854**, Cullowhee, NC: Western North Carolina University, 1953
- Rights, Douglas LeTell. **The American Indian in North Carolina**. Durham: Duke University Press, 1947.
- Rodenbough, Charles D. **Governor Alexander Martin**. Jefferson, NC: McFarland & Company, 2004.
- Rodenbough, Charles, **History of a Dream Deferred, William Byrd's Land of Eden**. Raleigh: Lulu Publishing, 2009
- Rodenbough, Charles, ed. **The Heritage History of Rockingham County**. Winston Salem: Hunter Publishing Company, 1983.
- Rowland, Dunbar, **Courts, Judges, and Lawyers of Mississippi 1798-1933**, Jackson, MS: State Department of Archives and History, 1935.
- Royster, Charles. **The Fabulous History of the Dismal Swamp Company**. New York: Alfred A. Knopf, 1999.
- Saunders, Richard R., compiled, **Open Doors and Closed Windows**, Reidsville: 1948

- Scarborough, William Kauffman. **The Overseer, Plantation Management in the Old South**. Athens: The University of Georgia Press, 1984.
- Scott, Hugh Reid, **History of the Settles, Reids, and Scotts**, Unpublished manuscript, Rockingham County Collection, RCC, Wentworth, NC
- Taylor, Rosser Howard, **Slaveholding in North Carolina, An Economic View**, New York: Negro Universities Press, 1926
- Tourgée, Albion Winegar, **The Invisible Empire**, Baton Rouge: The Louisiana State University Press, 1989
- Trelease, Allen W., **North Carolina Railroad 1849-1871**, Chapel Hill: The University of North Carolina Press, 1991
- Turner, Herbert Snipes. **The Dreamer, Archibald DeBow Murphey,1772-1832**. Verona, VA: McClure Publishing, 1971.
- Tyler, Rosser Howard. **Slave Holding in North Carolina**. New York: Negro University Press, 1969, reprint.
- Wellman, Manley Wade & Elizabeth Amis Cameron Wood, Blanchard. **The Life and Times of Sir Archie**. Chapel Hill: The University of North Carolina Press, 1958.
- Wheeler, John H. **Reminiscences and Memories of North Carolina and Eminent North Carolinians**, Baltimore: Genealogical Publishing Company, 1969 reprint of 1878
- Wiencek, Henry, **The Hairstons, An American Family in Black and White**. New York, St. Martin's Press, 1999.

ARTICLES

Butler, Lindley S. "Sauratown Plantation," The Rockingham County Journal of History and Genealogy, 8 (December 1983).hereafter JRCHG

Carter, Robert W., Jr., ed. "Leaksville of 'Ye Olden Times.'" JRCHG, 5 (June 1980)

Carter, Robert W., Jr., "Reflections on the Settle Family Cemetery." XVIV (December 1994) Number 2, 85

Carter, Robert W., Jr., "The Settle Cemetery Recording," XVIV, JRCHG (December 1994) Number 2, 87

Carter, Robert W., Jr., "Brief History of the Reuben Reid

Douglas, Dick, "Dick & Dillard Law School," remarks by R. D. Douglas, Jr., at the unveiling of an Historical Marker at the Law School location, April 24, 2008.

Douglas, Robert Dick Douglas, Jr., "Impeaching North Carolina Supreme Court Justices a Hundred Years Ago," The North Carolina State Bar Journal, 2011.

Family Cemetery," XVIV, JRCHG (December 1994) Number 2, 90

Hoover, Don, compiled by "Rockingham County, North Carolina 1800." JRCHG, XVIII (December 1992) Number 2, 45

Hoover, Don, Compiled by, "The Reuben Reid Cemetery Recording," XVIV, JRCHG (December 1994) Number 2, 97

Osburn, Mary E., transcribed by, "The Martin-Douglas Letters, Part Two." JRCHG, XVIV (December 1994) Number 2, 53

Perdue, Michael, Abstracted, "Robert Martin and Mary Settle Martin: Last Wills." JRCHG, XVIV (December 1994) Number 2, 80

Rodenbough, Charles D. ".... and 100 negroes brought from Antigua." The Journal of Rockingham County History and Genealogy. 10, (June 1985)

NEWSPAPERS, JOURNALS, ELECTRIC MEDIA

Ancestry.com

      Nancy Ann Graves (1815-18923)

      Winfield Scott Settle (1841-1903)

      Elizabeth Alberson (Settle) (1850-1937)

      Josiah Thomas Settle (1850-1915)

      Thomas Josiah Settle (1878-1957)

      Nancy and Josiah Settle Marriage 1858

Caswell County Historical Association (ncccha.blogspot.com)

      Will of Jaosiah Settle (1799-1860)

      Lewis slave petition (1854)

      Caswell County: 1855 Slave Sale Petition

Voyages: The Trans-Atlantic Slave Trade Database

Cuddins (www.cuddins.com)

      Descendants of John Lanier

Find a Grave (www.findagrave.com)

      Washington Settle (1830-1846)

      Mary Bynum Glenn (Settle) (1840-1895)

      Tyre Glenn family - Yadkin County

      Tyre Glenn (1800-1875)

Genforum (http://genform.genealogy.com

      Settle Family Rockingham County NC 1800-1870

Graves Family (www.gravesfa.org/gen 115.htm

Greensboro Daily News, June 19, 1932, Harry Z. Tucker, "The Story of Lucinda and Martha Martin,"

Greensboro Record, January 1960, Jan Thomas, "Douglas Destiny Clear on Day of Birth

Leaksville Gazette, Job Printing.

Memphis People (www.memphishistory.com/People\ Josiah Thomas Settle)

NC ECHO (ncccha.blogspot.com) Caswell County Family Tree - Azariah Graves

Rootsweb. Ancestry.con-
Josiah Settle (1799-1869)

Josiah Thomas Settle (1850-1915)

Frances Lea Graves (Settle) (1807-1829)

Elizabeth Graves (Settle) (1827-1909)

Nancy Ann Graves (Settle) (ca 1815-1893)

Thomas Graves (1740-1799)

Rhoda Mullins (1768-1852)

Azariah Graves (1768-1850)

Sky Elers Roots (http://skyelersroots.yool.net)

Tennessee Virtual Archives http??teva.contentdm.oclc.org) Josiah Thomas Settle

The Journal of Rockingham County History and Genealogy

Wikipedia.com

Compromise of 1850

Stephen A. Douglas

Glenwood (Enon, NC)

Martinsville MS

Other books by CHARLES D. RODENBOUGH:

GOVERNOR ALEXANDER MARTIN, Biography of a North Carolina Revolutionary Statesman (2004)

PINE HOUSE, The Day Emancipation Dawned (2009)

HISTORY OF A DREAM DEFERRED, William Byrd's Land of Eden (2009)

IF THE LORD IS WILLING AND THE CREEK STAYS LOW, A novel based on the life and influence of Rev. David Caldwell and Rachel Craighead Caldwell (2010)

STEALING ANDREW JACKSON'S HEAD, Captain Samuel W. Dewey (2011)

WHAT WE LOST OF THE GREATEST GENERATION, Lt. Victor H. Idol, Jr. (2013)

UNDERSTANDING THE FLOW OF ANCESTRY - ANTIGUA, volume II of The SAURATOWN PROJECT, Interactive Series (2013)

UNDERSTANDING THE FLOW OF ANCESTRY - NORTH CAROLINA, volume III of The SAURATOWN PROJECT, Interactive Series (2013)